AF817406

FAST-TRACK YOUR BUSINESS

A CUSTOMER-CENTRIC APPROACH TO ACCELERATE MARKET GROWTH

LAURA PATTERSON

author of *Measure What Matters* and *Metrics in Action*

The Violetear Press

Published by The Violetear Press

The
Violetear
Press

Copyright © 2020 Laura Patterson

All rights reserved.

No part of this publication may be reproduced, stored in or introduced into a retrieval system, or transmitted, in any form, or by any means (electronic, mechanical, photocopying, recording, or otherwise), without the prior permission of the publisher except in the case of brief quotations embodied in critical articles and review.

All company, product and service names used in this book are for identification purposes only and remain the rights of the respective company. Use of these names, logos, and brands does not imply any affiliation or endorsement.

Book Cover and Interior Design by Monkey C Media
The Circle of Traction illustration by Kris Kinney
Copyedited by Adrienne Moch

First Edition
Printed in the United States of America
ISBN: 978-0-9710086-2-5 (paperback)
Library of Congress Control Number: 2019915529

REVIEWS FROM EXPERTS WE ADMIRE

"Too many marketers measure their effectivity by easy to quantify metrics, such as number of clicks, amount of leads, and place in the search engine search, that they forget the basic importance of customer focus in marketing. Laura is doing a great job taking us back to the fundamentals of marketing."

—Arie Brish, author of bestseller
Lay an Egg and Make Chicken Soup

"The most certain path to success for any business is true, organic growth driven by loyal customers. *Fast-Track Your Business* offers a detailed game plan for building a company-wide focus on the customer. In a world where every company claims to be customer-centric, Laura Patterson's book will help your company become one of the few that really is."

—Roger Dooley, author of
Friction–The Untapped Force That Can Be Your Most Powerful Advantage

"*Fast-Track Your Business* is a very worthwhile read. The idea of organic growth is one I whole-heartedly agree with and love the idea of tying it to a model like the Circle of Traction. A practical and useful book full of ideas any company can use to create profitable growth."

—Mitch Goozé, coauthor of *Value Acceleration: The Secrets to Building an Unbeatable Competitive Advantage*

"This is a vitally important book for marketers competing in an increasingly skeptical, distracted and crowded marketplace. It is filled with practical, proven advice that can separate your brand, increase customer trust and directly impact your organization's growth."

—Matt Heinz, president, Heinz Marketing
Host Sales Pipeline Radio

"Laura is the queen of marketing metrics. But with this book, *Fast-Track Your Business: A Customer-Centric Approach to Accelerate Market Growth*, she has stepped outside marketing to challenge all businesses to step up their game and grow, grow, grow."

—Theresa Kushner, coauthor of
B2B-Data-Driven Marketing: Sources, Uses, Results

"Laura Patterson has the top-down goods and the bottom-up savvy to help any sized organization understand, engage, and win customers. Her understanding of the psychology of people and organizations, her knowledge of processes and systems, and her wisdom about data have given her consulting superpowers. *Fast-Track Your Business* is a goldmine of insightful advice, a roadmap to efficiency and a practical, tactical set of instructions."

—Jim Sterne, author of *Artificial Intelligence for Marketing: Practical Applications*

Fast-Track Your Business is dedicated to all the mentors in my career who modeled the way for growth and all the companies we've been privileged to serve and help grow.

J.T.,
Thank you for
contributing to Fast-Track!
With gratitude,
Laura

CONTENTS

FOREWORD

Marketing has undergone a period of a renaissance over the last twenty years, with innovation in new communication channels such as the internet and mobile data, and in advanced methods for connecting with customers directly, including social media, content platforms, and online distribution channels.

These changes have sparked a renewed interest and understanding of marketing as a critical component to success and driven new research. Marketing teams are analyzing the data insights around the customer's buying journey, segmenting customers with more specificity, and measuring and acting on customer behaviors in ways that were not possible before.

This has also spawned entirely new areas of specialization and education, in subjects such as digital marketing, marketing analytics, and marketing management through online tools. These new areas have led to faster, broader, and more measurable marketing execution, but they have also created a tendency to focus on the customer outreach tools, channels, and marketing programs that may or may not lead to long-term sustainable growth.

As a technology executive with over thirty-five years of experiencc, I had a career path that led from partner relations and junior marketing roles to leading worldwide product marketing teams at some of the largest technology companies in the world; eventually, I founded and served as CEO for one of the leading ruggedized mobile computing device companies in the world. Over that time, I have seen good companies grow based on understanding and delivering on customer needs and I have seen good companies fall from shifting to other priorities such as quarterly profit needs for the equity markets or a desire to create a market rather than fulfill customer needs. I have come to understand that great companies satisfy customer wants and needs better than the competition. It's no simpler than that.

Smart, successful companies understand customer success requires knowing who their customers are (including their needs and wants), the ways to connect with customers, and how many customers there are. Most importantly, they understand that creating products and services that meet and exceed customers' expectations—with clear differentiation from the competition—is a customer-centric approach that can lead to long-term customer engagement and success.

This customer-centric approach creates sustainable relationships that provide the fertile ground for new products and new customer segments. It ultimately leads to growing category shares, increasing revenues, and more profit—but it isn't done through flashy social media campaigns and display ads (although those are important for messaging). It's done through understanding their customers and the market environment, developing products and services that deliver value for customers, and taking timely action based on results measurement. Long-term, sustainable success—providing value and customer-centric solutions—is called organic growth.

Many books address marketing approaches in a theoretical way, which helps readers understand the basic concepts, but they leave many gaps in understanding how to execute. This book introduces a framework for understanding and planning called The Circle of Traction. This model provides a specific direction and questions to ask on the journey to creating a successful, profitable, and growing company.

Laura Patterson leads the reader through the steps necessary to understand the product's customers, competitors, measures, and outcomes—all critical for every business seeking sustained organic growth. She focuses on the most important elements of a marketing plan to ensure the core elements of the business strategy are customer-focused and value-driven.

David Altounian, PhD
Associate Dean, The Bill Munday School of Business
MBA Program Director
Partner, Capital Factory

PREFACE

After decades of working in or with Business-to-Business (B2B) companies, we started to see more companies asking, "What's our exit plan?" and fewer companies asking, "What's our growth plan?" We believe growth, measured in terms of increased revenue, profit, and/or assets, should be the focus for every company. We believe strongly that companies achieving organic growth will far exceed those that try to cobble companies together using a mergers and acquisitions (M&A) strategy.

Organic growth is the rate a company expands through its own business activity. It requires companies to create competitive advantages, differentiate and innovate their product/service offerings, and home in on viable existing and new customer opportunities. John Cummings of Business Finance, who examined the differences in shareholder return and revenue growth of the S&P 500, found organic growth produces a better financial outcome. Organizations that excel at efficient organic growth see total shareholder returns of 20 – 28 percent and revenue growth of 13 percent compared to organizations deriving growth from M&A. Firms that are efficient at M&A typically see about 13 – 15 percent total shareholder returns and revenue growth of only 8 percent. The purpose of this book to ignite your passion for organic growth.

INTRODUCTION

"When you stop growing you start dying." This quote is credited to William S. Burroughs, a writer who hails from my hometown of St. Louis. While I'm not sure he intended this message for business, it certainly applies. Not long ago, KPMG, an audit, tax, and advisory services firm, wrote that, "Growth is one of the top agenda items for CEOs."[1] It went on to say that new technologies, changing regulations, sector convergence (such as the convergence of computing and communications), and evolving customer needs are all underlying reasons for the growth mandate. CEOs recognize they need their entire leadership team to be on board to achieve growth, especially their chief marketing officer (CMO). A study by CMO Council, a peer network of senior corporate marketing leaders and brand decision-makers, claimed that "almost 70 percent of CEOs now expect CMOs to lead revenue growth."[2] Achieving growth, especially organic growth, is far easier said than accomplished. More recently, a Gartner survey declared that "growth tops the list of CEO business priorities in 2018 and 2019."[3]

To meet board and shareholder expectations, companies often sacrifice what will create long-term sustainable growth for short-term P&L (profit and loss) performance. Revenue refers to funds received from the sale of goods and services. Growth concentrates on expansion, with the primary concern being market share and/or category ownership and then cash, even to the point of sacrificing near-term profit. You can probably think of companies who may yet to be profitable but are rapidly growing, such as Hulu, which has twenty-eight million subscribers (as of May 1, 2019), but as of that date has yet to be profitable.[4]

The opposite also holds true. It is possible to achieve revenue while falling behind in growth, which will ultimately lead to the end of the road. For example, in the first quarter of 2018, Time Warner Inc. reported a 37 percent increase in revenue,[5] but a 7.1 percent decline in growth quarter over quarter. As companies such as Roku and Hulu gain more traction, traditional broadcasting companies potentially face extinction—but disruption isn't the only means of impeding growth. In 2018, Sam's Club announced the closing of sixty-three stores[6] because it could not keep pace with the sales growth of its primary competitor, Costco.

It's All About Organic Growth and an Upstream Focus

Achieving and maintaining growth is a challenge. Many books have been written on the topic, including classics such as *Competitive Advantage: Creating and Sustaining Superior Performance* (1985) by Michael Porter, and *Blue Ocean Strategy*, published twenty years later by W. Chan Kim and Renée Mauborgne. The topic is timeless and always timely. When VisionEdge Marketing was founded in 1999, our focus was less on helping companies achieve near-term revenue and more on helping companies achieve long-term sustainable organic growth. This continues to be a primary focus of our company, and we developed a construct we call the Circle of Traction to support our work.

In 2018, Jim Obermeyer of the Sales Leadership Management Association (SLMA) offered me the opportunity to host a live radio show. I agreed as long as organic growth could be the focus of the show and the guests could be CEOs with proven growth track records.

This book is a result of our work and these conversations. It is the hope of our Austin-based company and my personal aspiration that it will help you accelerate your organic growth, which is growth achieved by your own internal efforts. This leads me to point out the use of personal pronouns in this book. The use of "I" refers to my personal experience or point of view, while the use of "we" refers to the expertise and work of VisionEdge Marketing. This book will not address growth where businesses transfer or consolidate with each other, which is the domain of mergers and acquisitions. There are numerous other books and resources should this route appeal to you.

In addition, the number of books and resources dedicated to downstream marketing, such as digital marketing, content marketing, social media marketing, event marketing, etc., are far too many to enumerate. Whether you search Amazon, Barnes & Noble, or Google, you'll find enough reading material on these topics to keep you and/or a Marketing team occupied for months. To paraphrase Dave Sikora, an Austin serial CEO, if the upstream is wrong then the downstream is polluted. We focus on the upstream.

Introducing the Circle of Traction

Before delving into what it takes to achieve organic growth, I'd like to introduce you to the VisionEdge Marketing Circle of Traction (Figure 1). We developed this wheel or what we call the Circle of Traction about twenty years ago and have modified it only slightly over the years. Let's examine each of the wheel's elements, since we've organized this book around it.

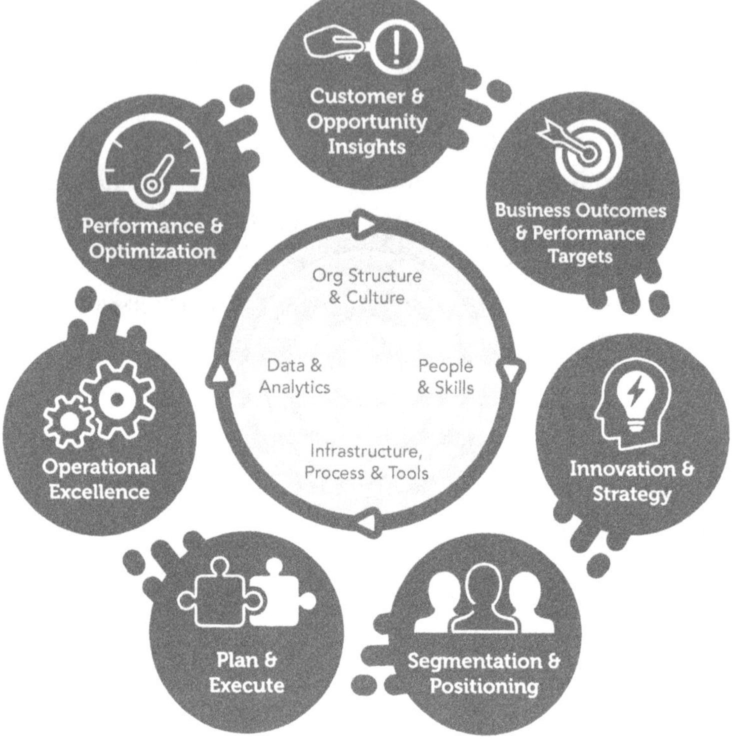

Figure 1: VisionEdge Marketing's Circle of Traction

All wheels need an axle, shaft, or spindle that enable them to turn and fulfill their function. The axle for the Circle of Traction consists of four components: Organizational Culture & Structure; People & Skills; Infrastructure, Process & Tools; and Data & Analytics. These are fundamental components; without them, the wheel won't turn. Most of Chapter 2, which is dedicated to these axle elements, focuses on Organizational Culture & Structure, because a growth culture sets the stage for everything else. When it comes to People & Skills, whether your people are on the inside or outside isn't as important as having the right people with the right skills, especially skills around data, strategy, and execution. As for Infrastructure, Process & Tools, every business runs on processes, as does Marketing. Tools without processes are a safety hazard. Process first then tools. We explore processes and operational excellence in more detail in Chapter 9. Finally, there's the Data & Analytics axle, which is critical to ensuring information collected can provide insights to facilitate better decisions and improved performance.

Each element on the outside of the Circle of Traction has its own chapter. All the content reflects the most necessary requirements and actions to achieve growth—focusing on the role of Marketing, especially upstream Marketing, which is explained in Chapter 1. (The capitalization of Marketing in this sentence and throughout this book is intentional. Read "Why and When to Capitalize Marketing" on page 12 to learn why.) Chapter 10 is of particular note, since it focuses on performance management, a discipline in its own right and one we helped pioneer for Marketing. A single chapter on the topic won't do it justice, but a book on organic growth wouldn't be complete without its inclusion.

As I said, I'm a native of St. Louis who landed in Texas. This makes for an interesting mix of practicality and exploratory. I've tried to keep the book practical and actionable. Lessons learned by CEOs and from our work are sprinkled throughout the book where relevant. Takeaways are included at the end of each chapter. We welcome engaging in a conversation with you along the way, so feel free to reach out directly or via our various social media channels.

WHY AND WHEN TO CAPITALIZE MARKETING

Quite a few years ago, we had an intense debate within VisionEdge Marketing over my insistence on capitalizing the word "Marketing." You're probably laughing right now, thinking what a waste of energy and effort. Or maybe you're thinking what's in the water in Texas? In looking back, however, this turned out to be an extremely important conversation for us. I hope it will spark a similar conversation around your table. Let me share a bit more about our discussion.

As part of the debate, one of our team members with a strong journalistic background pointed out that capitalization is only for proper nouns. She brought up the example, "We are marketing our new product," and I conceded using the word "marketing" as a verb shouldn't be capitalized. Ah, the team thought it had me and got on a roll. Another person popped up with this phrase, "We're going to finance our new car." In this example, finance is used as a verb, and yes, it does not need to be capitalized.

You might be thinking, end of discussion—what more is there to talk about? Turns out that those examples, inadvertently, began to help crystallize our thinking about when to capitalize Marketing. As the conversation ensued, we easily agreed that when we designate a particular place or thing, we have a proper noun. When we reference Marketing as a function, it's a particular thing. Therefore, in these instances, it makes sense to capitalize it.

With this in mind, we began capitalizing Marketing when used as a reference to the Marketing department, the Marketing function, the Marketing organization, etc. or it's assumed this is the reference. Also, we agreed this would hold true for any function within a company, and so we began to apply the capitalization rule there as well (Finance goals, etc.).

As we began to explore the nuances of the distinction between function and activity, we realized the work of the Marketing function should be far too important to the success of a company to relegate it to something perceived as inconsequential. When Marketing is playing a pivotal and strategic role, it deserves to be capitalized. When it isn't, well, it isn't. Day-to-day marketing doesn't merit capitalization. Deliberate value-creating growth-accelerating Marketing action does.

Your Marketing organization earns the capital when it delivers on the upstream and downstream. Every organization needs a Marketing function that effectively performs both.

We don't always get the capitalization right. However, we'd rather err on the side of capitalizing what we believe is one of the most important functions within any organization than subjugate it to a subordinate role. If we want the Marketing discipline to lead the organization to success, it cannot be in a subordinate position. This idea has significant implications for the discipline. It means we must take responsibility for more than generating leads/contacts, implementing campaigns, and supporting the Sales function. It means we must oversee accelerating growth and creating value.

It's our point of view that Marketing must bring strategy or strategies to the table based on data-derived insights that help the organization navigate and realize the desired future-state. When Marketing performs this role and fulfills its fundamental mission, we believe it's worthy of capitalization. That's why we care, and we hope you do, too.

Customer & Opportunity Insights
Business Outcomes & Performance Targets
Innovation & Strategy
Segmentation & Positioning
Plan & Execute
Operational Excellence
Performance & Optimization
Org Structure & Culture
People & Skills
Infrastructure, Process & Tools
Data & Analytics

CHAPTER 1

UPSTREAM MARKETING

THE PATH TO LONG-TERM ORGANIC GROWTH

Because we strongly believe companies need to be customer-centric, a topic we'll delve more deeply into, the wheel begins with insights based on customer, market, and competitive intelligence. These insights help businesses decide where to place their best and extend their victories, as well as what to protect or jettison. Armed with these decisions, organizations can determine what they need to accomplish to declare success. These outcomes are what enable organizations to achieve their financial targets.

Once outcomes are defined ideally in customer-centric terms—where your customers rather than your product are at the core of your business—you can craft strategies, innovate, and position solutions that will address customer needs, create customer value, and achieve customer success within the market segments where you can best compete. These first few spokes of the wheel fall squarely in what we refer to as upstream Marketing.

In his book, *Profitable Growth is Everyone's Business,* Dr. Ram Chara, who has taught at Boston University, Northwestern University, and Harvard's Business School, explains the difference between upstream and downstream Marketing. Upstream Marketing, Dr. Chara says, refers to "the strategic process of identifying and fulfilling customer needs." He posits that developing clear customer segments, along with analyzing how the customer uses the product or service and what competitive advantage will be required to acquire the customer, are the focus of upstream Marketing.

Dr. Chara defines downstream Marketing as efforts such as advertising, promotion, brand building, and other forms of communication and engagement, including PR, events, and content. He proposes that the purpose of these efforts is to motivate customers to adopt existing products and services. Perhaps this helps clarify the difference. Downstream Marketing supports your company's value proposition, while upstream Marketing defines your company's value proposition. Downstream Marketing delivers programs to support product adoption. Upstream Marketing directs the innovation process to ensure long-term sustainable growth.

Upstream includes everything from deciding which markets and customers to pursue, what method is needed, and where and when to pursue to what offers and messaging to use. Upstream Marketing requires a longer-term investment and keen focus on performance management. It also requires delving into a different level of data—gaining deep customer insights and competitive intelligence by investing in research; understanding the principles of segmentation, positioning, and differentiation; and distilling this into a strategy and plan for growth that is aligned to the business. If you're looking for long-term organic growth—which requires innovation, category ownership, and customer lifetime value to build a business that lasts—you need to invest in the upstream.

Upstream Capability Requirements

Upstream Marketing is what earns Marketing the capital "M." (Did you read "Why and When to Capitalize Marketing" in the

Introduction?) Marketing organizations that earn the capital have four distinct capabilities:

1. **They understand the needs and wants of the market and customers.** I remember a mentor years ago telling me "it is better to be an aspirin than a vitamin." Upstream Marketing aims to solve headaches and know which headaches go with which market segments. This requires conducting formal and informal research—the focus of our next chapter. Research starts with a hypothesis or educated guess. A hypothesis typically takes the form of a question that surfaces as a result of observation, e.g., we're not seeing the adoption rate of our product or service as we anticipated, so what do we need to address to improve—feature set, messaging, delivery, etc.? Which one of these will have the greatest impact on the rate? You might even have an initial theory, such as you may believe an additional function or capability will improve the rate of adoption. The only way to verify your guesses is to conduct experiments, analyze your data, and draw conclusions from it. This approach can be used for nearly every aspect of Marketing, such as a hypothesis that customers prefer a particular medium for learning about your products or a specific option for getting help when they're having trouble solving a problem. Being able to frame the question takes collecting data—talk with prospects; attend industry events; and read, read, and read some more (industry articles, analyst reports, experts' blogs, etc.). We live in a dynamic world where needs change. For example, Kodak never evolved to embrace digital photography. Blockbuster (and all video rental stores) couldn't compete with on-demand options such as Netflix. Or consider the Toys 'R Us stores closing as they tried unsuccessfully to compete with online and big-box stores. Your research needs to be ongoing so you can zig and zag with the market. It's the only way to avoid the fate of these failed brands.

2. **They gather and validate the market requirements to create innovation—differentiated solutions, features, and benefits that will resonate with buyers.** What is the minimal feature set your offer needs to ease the headache? Of course, everything about your offer matters to you. The key is to focus on what matters to your customers. Focus is paramount. Drill down on the one or two most important differentiated benefits. Note the word "benefits"—upstream Marketing speaks from benefits, not features. Features are your evidence. Consider employing a new product development (NPD) process, such as Stage-Gate, as part of this process. It prepares and implements a launch plan that will entice customers to purchase. The launch plan should be prepared well in advance of the launch and is just as necessary as any of the main features of the new product. We tackle this capability in Chapters 5 and 6, which focus on the all-important wheel element of Innovation & Strategy.

3. **They determine the personas of buyers and approach segmentation beyond the traditional methods of demographics.** This capability takes more than monitoring social media platforms to develop personas. Conversations with buyers are your best source for personas. This means Marketing must engage directly with customers—ideally in person. This step isn't about pitching; it's about listening to customers and learning about their problems, challenges, aspirations, etc. Pay close attention to the words they use. Their language needs to become your language. This is the focus of Chapter 7, which addresses the Segmentation & Positioning element.

4. **They recognize that Marketing must be agile and facilitate agility**. The market research company Forrester defines business agility as "the quality that allows an enterprise to embrace market and operational changes as a matter of

routine." Achieving agility depends on operational and performance excellence—which are addressed in the final chapters—and it requires building the infrastructure and activating processes, systems, and tools. The benefit of doing this at any organization is that it helps you increase the execution speed of your business.

Upstream and Downstream Coexist

Clearly, you need both upstream and downstream Marketing, and a way to pivot from one to the other. Routes-to-Market (RTM) and your Operational Plan become the transitional spokes between the two. Execution is all about the downstream, with measures, metrics, and Key Performance Indicators (KPIs) derived from the outcomes, strategies, and plans. Downstream is all about the execution. Downstream Marketing suits the world we operate in: sales NOW. It plays to the call for fast ROI. It is about speed and financial management. The downside is that without being grounded to the upstream, the downstream Marketing budget is always at risk.

As the plan is executed and performance data captured, an organization can assess whether to stay or adjust course and what additional insights are needed to stay or accelerate the growth trajectory. Thus, the wheel continues to spin—upstream Marketing building the momentum for its downstream counterpart.

Achieving Organic Growth via Marketing

We hope the wheel helps you understand the importance and power of upstream Marketing to the growth process. We truly believe Marketing should take the lead for successfully achieving organic growth. While corporate leaders need to drive the organic growth initiative, Marketing plays a defining and major role. Identifying markets and customers to pursue falls squarely in Marketing's domain. It is Marketing that can provide the insight and guidance to answer questions such as whether the opportunity present is to grow share of wallet among existing customers by offering more ancillary products or developing a new offering to penetrate a new market and attract new customers.

Value-creating marketers see themselves in the business of creating new benefits for current customers, finding new customers for existing products, and driving innovations that will keep their business ahead of the competition.

As the pressure for companies to improve organic growth increases, Marketing is in the ideal position to step up and take the lead by developing and orchestrating a disciplined process for selecting the best organic growth initiatives. The Circle of Traction is one tool. Ultimately, however, Marketing is going to need a way to identify and select the best options for organic growth. A useful approach is to begin with a realistic assessment of the gap(s) between the goals for growth and current rate of growth based on current strategy plus the projects already in the portfolio of growth initiatives. Will the current sources of growth close the gap? If the answer is no, you can put the Circle of Traction in motion. It's designed to help you focus on answering these important questions:

- What do you need to know about your markets, customers, and competitors that will help you close the gap?
- Can you close the gap by penetrating deeper into your current customer base or market?
- Can you do this with your existing product/service portfolio?
- Do you need to innovate or go into new markets? How real is the opportunity? In what time frame? What is your likelihood of success and how much is the opportunity worth?

- Do you have the market's permission to grow this way?

How you answer these questions will help you define your priorities and how success will be determined. These two things serve as the basis to establishing your business outcomes and the corresponding strategies you will need to develop and deploy.

TAKEAWAYS

- Upstream Marketing defines your company's value proposition and focuses on solving market and customer problems to ensure long-term sustainable growth.
- To be successful using upstream Marketing, you must understand the needs and wants of your market and customers, gather and validate market requirements to create customer value, understand personas beyond traditional demographics or firmographics, and recognize the need for Marketing to be agile.
- Downstream Marketing supports your company's value proposition and delivers programs to support adoption of your product or service.
- You need downstream and upstream Marketing in your quest for organic growth.

TEN QUESTIONS THAT NEED TO BE ANSWERED AS PART OF UPSTREAM MARKETING

The waters upstream may feel more turbulent and murkier, but it's really where a foundational part of Marketing exists. Want to wade deeper in upstream Marketing? Start by addressing these ten questions:

- What will our customers want next?
- How would we deliver what our customers want next?
- How will we convert this into a competitive advantage?
- Where is the market moving?
- How do we want to participate in these moves?
- What customers do we want next?
- Where will we find them?
- What will they value?
- What is our roadmap for developing future products that deliver this value?
- How will we bring these new products to the market?

The answers to these questions are vitally important because they fuel growth. But, never forget that when it comes time to execute the plan derived from your upstream efforts, you're going to need solid downstream skills.

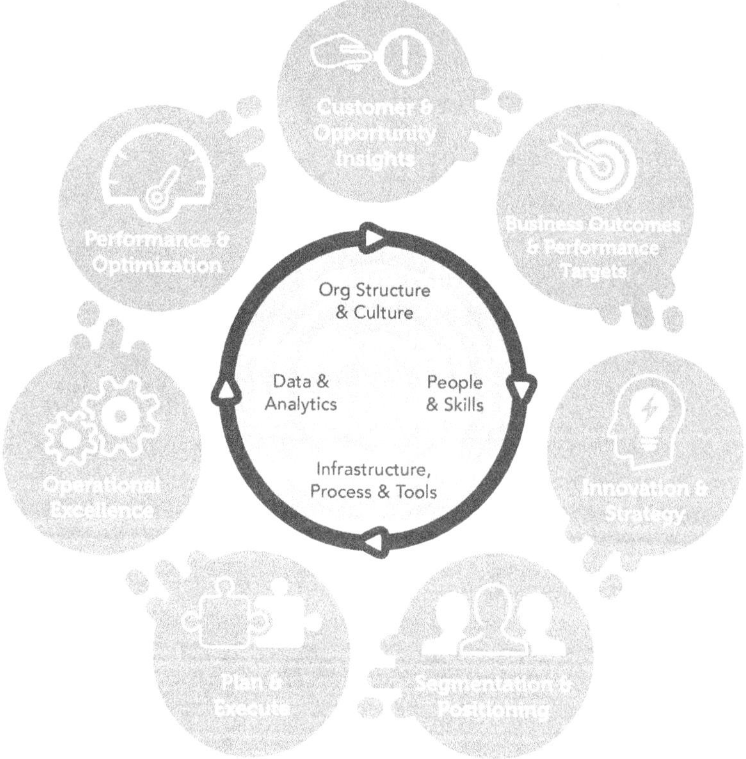
Customer & Opportunity Insights
Business Outcomes & Performance Targets
Innovation & Strategy
Segmentation & Positioning
Plan & Execute
Operational Excellence
Performance & Optimization
Org Structure & Culture
People & Skills
Infrastructure, Process & Tools
Data & Analytics

CHAPTER 2

THE AXLE ELEMENTS

IT ALL STARTS WITH CULTURE

Without an axle, your car won't be able to move. Axle assemblies consist of a variety of parts, such as a hub allowing for rotation, a constant velocity (CV) joint to facilitate constant rotational speed without an appreciable increase in friction or play, and a driveshaft to transfer the power of the engine to the wheels. The axle must be able to sustain the entire weight of the vehicle and withstand the accelerated forces of driving and braking, which are of course controlled by the driver. This axle concept also applies to the Circle of Traction, which has an axle comprised of four primary components: culture (the hub); infrastructure, process, and tools (the CV joint); data and analytics (the driveshaft); and people and skills (the driver). While the latter component—having the right people with the right skills—is an absolute necessity for any organization to move forward, without a hub, the wheel cannot turn, hence the importance of culture and the primary focus of this chapter.

Culture. Every leader talks about it. Every company has one. As mentioned in the introduction, CEOs are under increasing pressure to achieve growth. Culture is the one vital variable a CEO influences that will either drive or disrupt an organization's overall growth. Despite businesses jockeying to be ahead on the growth curve, Janet Yung in her book, *Being Happy and Successful–The Entrepreneur in You*, states that most businesses fall short of achieving their growth objectives for revenue and profitability. She purports that success rates are as low as 20 percent. A large part of this shortcoming is due to the lack of growth-oriented organizational cultures. If growth is one of your key imperatives, you must define and build a culture that will help fuel it.

Before we can discuss how to create a culture for growth, we must first define company culture. The *Merriam Webster Dictionary* provides a useful definition: "The set of shared attitudes, values, goals, and practices that characterizes an institution or organization." Culture reflects the socially transmitted behavior patterns that mirror how a group of people operate. It emerges and evolves wherever groups of people congregate—including where we work. An organization's culture reflects the way its workers think, behave, work, and interact. It can guide, inspire, and motivate or do just the opposite. Culture also affects how well an organization attracts and retains employees, partners, and customers.

Unsurprisingly, a company's goals, structure, and philosophies communicate its culture. A study by Kronos, *Who's the Boss of Workplace Culture?*, found that "human resources (HR) professionals, people managers, and employees have very different opinions about workplace culture, who drives it, what's important to creating a great one, and what can destroy workplace culture."[7] Traditionally, culture fell under the auspices of the HR function. However, many organizations no longer have separate HR and Organizational Development departments. In organizations where HR exists on its own, this function may be responsible for executing the culture, but ultimately it's the responsibility of the CEO to create and drive it.

You know from experience that organizational cultures vary. For example, perhaps today you're in an organization where the culture encourages employees to see themselves as family members, with a focus on mentoring, nurturing, and "doing things together." Another culture might primarily be entrepreneurial, with a focus on risk-taking, innovation, and "doing things first." Perhaps you know of an organization whose culture is results-oriented, with a focus on competition, achievement, and "getting the job done." Or maybe one that has a more hierarchical culture, where process, efficiency, and structure—that is, "doing things right"—are the essential behaviors.

Regardless, it's the CEO who creates and nurtures a culture of growth. To foster such a culture, the CEO must first define the organization's values and expected behaviors. Ideally, these values will spring from and support the company's purpose while being applicable to everyone within the organization. A company's purpose is derived from its values. (David Friedman describes thirty core values in his book, *Fundamentally Different.*)

In our work, we've found there are two keys to developing a growth culture: making it real, and protecting and nurturing it.

Make it real. Document your values and the corresponding behaviors. Describe your culture so every employee understands the associated principles, goals, and values. All members of your organization need to know the specific behaviors you expect them to exhibit. To accomplish this efficiently, consider incorporating a culture statement into your strategic plan, business reviews, and employee reviews. Additionally, you should require your leadership team to embody and propagate the desired workplace culture. Furthermore, explore how to translate your company's culture statement into content you're willing to share with customers and have included in the public domain via your website and social media platforms. For example, if collaboration is a key value, then what that means and how it's manifested needs to permeate across the organization—internally and externally. Internally, this might mean employees work in cross-functional teams. Externally, this might impact how you work with suppliers.

Protect and nurture it. As you grow and add people and suppliers to your team, your culture is at risk. After all, the more people involved, the greater the opportunity for dilution. To help curb this effect, recruit with your culture in mind and hire people whose values and behaviors match yours. Write down all the qualities you think prospective employees and suppliers need and the behaviors you consider essential. Incorporate this information into your job descriptions and supplier contracts. For example, if responsiveness is an essential behavior to support your culture, be clear what that means behaviorally. For example, the VP of our business unit in a company I previously worked for was adamant that all phone calls were returned by the end of the business day. This requirement was a crystal-clear behavioral representation of his desire to cultivate a culture of responsiveness.

Focus on Solving Customer Problems

What are some of the characteristics of a culture of growth? Growth cultures tend to be customer-centric and focused. The culture is growth-centric while still emphasizing the need for a deep understanding of customers' wants and needs. These cultures align their organization around customer engagement, experience, and long-term success. In 2010, Ranjay Gulati wrote *Reorganize for Resilience: Putting Customers at the Center of Your Business*. Based on ten years of research, Gulati found that when companies made products based on what customers need and want, they were more successful. Today, we live in the "Age of the Customer"[8] in an "Engagement Economy."[9] Companies with a culture oriented toward solving customer problems are more likely to succeed.

The bigger the business problem, the more urgent, and the better your offer addresses the problem, the more likely and faster you are to create and acquire customers and grow. Therefore, a key part of any customer-centric business focused on growth is to be clear about the problem you solve. Creating a solution before identifying the problem can have devastating consequences, which is why the innovation and strategy chapter comes after the chapters devoted to customer and opportunity insights and business outcomes and performance targets. Even if you're convinced you have the next best idea ever, it's always a good idea to validate there is a need in the market. You may still decide to pursue your idea even if the market doesn't completely embrace your innovation. Keep in mind that people might have opted for a better horse and buggy if Benz and Ford hadn't persevered with the automobile.

Determining the need for your offer doesn't always require sophisticated research. I'll use the birth of our company to illustrate this point. In 1999, a colleague and I were receiving tons of calls from local firms looking for Marketing help. It made us wonder whether there was an opportunity to build our own firm. We decided to use these conversations to determine whether to pursue the idea of our firm further.

As we engaged with these callers, we started asking more questions about the challenges they were facing. Did they just need more people, or did they have real challenges and problems to solve? Topics we discussed included the need for clearer product definition, messaging, and positioning; better competitive intelligence and customer information to improve go-to-market strategy, targeting, and measurement of Marketing; and improved and in some cases the development of Marketing processes. Ah, we thought, that's why our backgrounds in research/data/analytics, measurement, and operations are important. Now that we understood the problems, we probed further to try and learn how important it was for them to solve them—did they just want it or did they truly need it? Turns out, it was important then and it remains important today. These two recurring themes—the desire to be more customer-centric and the desire to make more data-derived decisions—persist today, hence the creation and growth of VisionEdge Marketing.

The point of the story is that the first step to growth for successful companies is to solve problems. For your organization to position itself and develop a compelling value proposition, you must be able to clearly articulate the problem(s) and understand how you are better and different from alternatives, including the alternative of doing nothing. This requires a culture that has an insatiable appetite for learning about your market and customers' problems and the magnitude of these problems. (Yes, it always comes back to culture.)

Data, Data, and More Data

Knowing what customers need and want takes data. While data is highly prized within modern companies, having a growth culture allows you to avoid succumbing to analysis-paralysis by promoting a decisive and execution-oriented approach to numbers. Speaking of numbers and data, growth cultures often reflect a data- and performance-driven culture because growth cultures are typically focused on results. Growth cultures focus on converting the insights into action that facilitates growth, creates customer value, and improves performance.

It will be essential for your Marketing organization to embrace a data-driven culture. A data-to-insights culture is data-driven—a culture that thrives on getting the most out of its analytics-to-action processes. In its Business of Data report[10], *The Economist's* Intelligence Unit rated companies that are ahead of their competitors in the use of data as three times more likely to be financially successful. These companies rely on data-driven decision-making over intuition or experience. You can tell when you're in a data-to-insights culture when the organization employs a consistent, repeatable approach to using data to make tactical and strategic decisions.

Achieving a data-to-insights culture in Marketing requires the Marketing organization to have the right tools, quality data, a data inventory, access to the data, data literacy, and processes to harvest and analyze the data. Armed with these capabilities, Marketing organizations are better positioned to either directly act on the data by developing and implementing Marketing initiatives that have the greatest likelihood of success, rather than just "winging it" or using intuition. These teams can also use data to measure the success of such initiatives, adjusting and optimizing strategy and programs to ensure achievement of goals.

Never Forget About Customers

One more attribute is worth highlighting before we wrap up this chapter. Growth cultures recognize long-term success depends on keeping and growing the value of customers and having customers become fans and advocates. For this to occur, a growth culture must be customer-centric and focused. This means customer success, service, and experience are fundamental values of the culture. In the words of Nick Mehta, CEO of Gainsight, "The success of your business is inherently intertwined with the success of your customer."

None of us has a business if we don't have customers. Customer support, strategic account management, and customer success all aim to retain, nurture, and grow customer relationships by helping your customers gain more value from your company. While there may be a variety of definitions around customer success, we like the one from the Customer Success Association, which defines customer success as "a long-term, scientifically engineered, and professionally directed strategy for maximizing customer and company sustainable proven value."[11] This definition helps differentiate customer success from customer support. Customer support is reactive, solving customer problems as they arise. Customer success is proactive—and creating and delivering superior value over the long term is how you keep and grow your customers. Customer success is a directed strategy focused on value, value for both the customer and your company. Therefore, the key to customer success and a function of supporting it is understanding two things:

- What's of value to your customers
- What *your* value is to your customers

Closely associated with customer success is customer experience. Gartner, in its May 2018 *Customer Experience (CX) in Marketing Survey*,[12] reported that more than two-thirds of the respondents said their companies compete mostly based on customer experience (CX), and 81 percent say in two years, they expect to be competing mostly or completely on the basis of CX. It's no wonder then, that optimizing CX is the number one opportunity for many organizations, according to Adobe's Digital Trends 2018 Report.[13] And, there is a good financial reason to invest in improving the customer experience. The Global Customer Experience Benchmarking study[14] by Dimension Data, conducted in 2019, found that 84 percent of organizations working to improve CX have experienced an increase in revenue.

What is CX and how can you improve it? Forrester defines customer experience as "how customers perceive their interactions with your company."[15] We prefer this definition for CX: "The sum of all experiences a customer has with a supplier of goods and/or services, over the duration of their relationship with that supplier. This can include awareness, discovery, attraction, interaction, purchase, use, cultivation, and advocacy."[16] Essentially, CX is the entire experience through which we satisfy customers' needs and create value. These individual interactions occur across your company throughout your customer's lifetime. Over thirty years ago, Jan Carlzon, former CEO of SAS Airlines, wrote a book called *Moments of Truth*. He defined a moment of truth, "as any interaction with a customer or any event in which a customer uses or experiences a company's product." How employees handle a moment of truth has a significant impact on customer satisfaction, retention, and advocacy. Employees are the keepers of moments of truth. This is why CX, service quality, and customer success are all inextricably linked and must be ingrained within the culture.

Rob Fields, a cultural curator, believes, "culture is the one thing that enables marketers to create greater engagement, relevance, and grow their business. The failure to acknowledge the importance of culture to brand- and business-building is the same as deciding that you're okay with being at a competitive disadvantage." To translate this, Fields is underscoring the fact that the culture you have inside your company will be outwardly reflected in the interactions your employees have with customers. This is a critical reminder, because your customers' experience is the ultimate expression of your brand. Echoing Carlzon, he notes that the interactions between your customers and your company are the moments of truth that form lasting impressions. Therefore, as one of the primary customer-facing functions of your organization, Marketing will inevitably mirror the internal culture. So, no matter what your growth strategies, they will only spur success if you create and perpetuate a culture of growth.

Build a culture that's passionate about service quality, one where employees are empowered to own moments of truth, and you'll be well on your way to growth. Churn will be less of an issue and referrals will be greater if your company is fanatical about service quality. A small example is just being able to reach a person or have a problem quickly resolved. With the advent of automated voice response and chatbots, many companies have forgotten the power of the human touch. In some companies, I often never reach a real person unless I select the sales or billing option. More and more companies are encouraging you to use their website help center for support rather than talking with a person. Master the service basics that contribute to customer success. We recommend the book, *Delivering on Service Quality*, written by Valerie Zeithaml and first published in 1990. Reliability, responsiveness, and empathy will go a long way toward keeping and growing the value of your customers and earning you a thumbs up reputation.

While we can't provide an exhaustive list of attributes associated with growth cultures, the traits outlined here appear to exist within every successful one we've ever encountered. When you cultivate this type of culture, the entire team can then focus on facilitating business growth and creating customer value. Your axle will be well lubricated and ready to drive you forward.

TAKEAWAYS

- If organic growth is one of your key imperatives, you must define and build a culture that will help fuel it.
- Companies with a culture oriented toward solving customer problems are more likely to succeed.
- Growth cultures are data- and performance-oriented, because they are typically focused on results.
- Organic growth cultures recognize long-term success depends on keeping and growing the value of customers and having customers become fans and advocates.

CULTURE AS A GROWTH DRIVER IN ACTION

Scribe Media, led by president and CEO JT McCormick, says it all comes down to culture: "We hire for culture fit first, skill set second. And that's the driver behind what we do. Our number one principle and value is results." Focusing on culture as a growth driver is working for Scribe Media. Founded in 2014, just five years later, Scribe Media is a profitable, growing company that has worked with more than 750 authors. If you wonder whether culture is relevant, the firm was recently ranked in its category as the second best company to work at in Austin.

This isn't the first time JT's focused on culture. Before Scribe Media, he was the president of Headspring Software, which he helped grow into a multimillion-dollar company with more than one hundred employees that was repeatedly ranked as one of the best places to work in all of Texas. JT understands grit on both the business and personal front. He tells his personal journey in his book, *I Got There: How I Overcame Racism, Poverty, and Abuse to Achieve the American Dream*, which tells the story of how he worked his way out of poverty, starting his career cleaning toilets and eventually becoming the president of multiple companies.

In my conversation with JT, he emphasized that "growth is at the top of our list, and we are achieving it organically. We have no outside capital. So, there's no debt, no loans, no venture capital, no private equity. We believe in organic. It's at the top of our list for us as far as growth is concerned." JT believes that "Marketing plays the No. 1 role for growth for our company. We have no outbound sales. Marketing drives the business and our innovation."

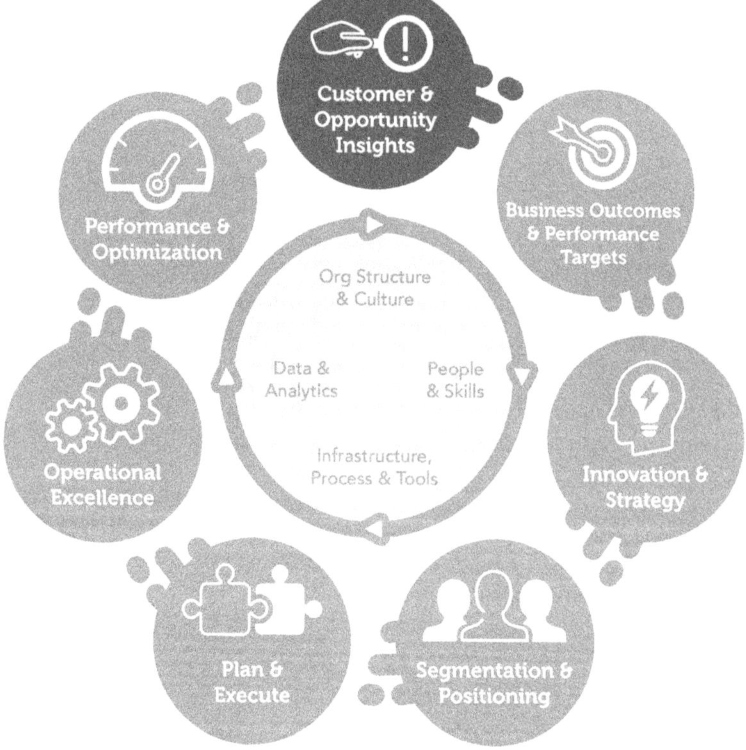
Customer & Opportunity Insights
Business Outcomes & Performance Targets
Innovation & Strategy
Segmentation & Positioning
Plan & Execute
Operational Excellence
Performance & Optimization
Org Structure & Culture
People & Skills
Infrastructure, Process & Tools
Data & Analytics

CHAPTER 3

CUSTOMER & OPPORTUNITY INSIGHTS

KNOW YOUR CUSTOMER, MARKET, AND COMPETITION

Increasing in size or substance is the definition of growth. You can't approach market growth—that is, increasing your size and substance in the market where you wish to compete—with random acts of effort and energy. To grow, you need a deliberate approach that will enable you to move forward faster and with more force.

You can burn a lot of energy (calories) and use a lot of effort (heart rate) running in place, but you won't have covered much distance. However, when you step forward and apply effort and energy, you'll travel some amount of distance over some period of time. Climb on a bicycle and exert the same effort and energy as you did while running and you'll go farther in the same amount of time or cover the same distance faster.

This is the inherent value of a wheel—to remove friction, facilitate movement, and magnify force. In simple terms, wheels help us harness energy, in everything from bicycles and cars to windmills, turbines, and more.

In the words of automotive writer Miles Cook, "You can have the most powerful engine, the most sophisticated transmission, the most elaborate super-trick suspension, and every other automotive widget known to mankind, but it all ain't worth a tinker's damn if the wheels are subpar."[17]

A spoked wheel goes one step further—it provides strength. Spokes transfer the energy from the hub to the wheel.

The Circle of Traction, your wheel to organic growth, is comprised of seven spokes. The wheel itself will give you traction and facilitate speed. When you execute the seven elements in the order recommended, you'll create momentum—moving faster in a specific direction. The first spoke in the Circle of Traction is Customer & Opportunity Insights.

Do You Have a Market?

We truly believe that understanding how you're going to make a difference in the market and create value for your customers is the fundamental question for every business professional. In the words of Richard Branson of Virgin, "Business people have to think about how their business can actually better this world."[18]

New ideas, good ideas, and creative ideas are all awesome, but to be worthy they must be wanted and needed by the market. It's also easy to be lured by a hot trend or the latest cool idea. Gone are the days of making business decisions, including growth decisions, solely based on your gut, intuition, or experience. You need answers to questions such as these to make data-derived growth decisions:

- What is the problem in the market?
- How big is the problem?
- Who and how many have it?
- How many people are trying to close this gap?

- What will be the difference before versus after the problem is solved?
- Why hasn't the problem already been solved?

Insights derived from data are the currency to today's decisions. Insights-driven businesses are growing at an average of more than 30 percent each year, and by 2020 are predicted to take $1.8 trillion annually from their less-informed peers, notes the Forrester *Insights-Driven Businesses Set the Pace for Global Growth* report.[19] According to the MicroStrategy 2018 *Global State of Enterprise Analytics Report*,[20] which surveyed 500 analytics and business intelligence decision-makers from around the world, respondents fostering a data-driven business are seeing these seven key benefits:

- Improved efficiency and productivity: 63 percent
- Faster, more effective decision-making: 57 percent
- Better financial performance: 51 percent
- Competitive advantage: 48 percent
- Improved customer experience: 48 percent
- Improved customer acquisition and retention: 46 percent
- Identification and creation of new revenue streams: 43 percent

Data is plentiful; the sheer volume of it presents more opportunities and challenges than ever before. Insights, however, aren't as abundant—and business leaders depend on the insights derived from data to make strategic growth decisions. Marketing is in the ideal position to harness data, whether it's customer data, market data, or competitive intelligence. The power of the customer-centric organization lies in being able to decipher data. Having the ability to derive valuable insights from data—especially customer insights—is what sets organizations and their Marketing teams apart from the rest of the pack.

The concept of a supply chain is ideal for tackling the challenge of converting raw data into actionable insights. Supply chains convert raw materials—in this case data—into a product—in this case insights—that can be stored and distributed to various interdependent members of the "network," such as Marketing, Sales, Service, R&D, etc., to give your customers what they want, when, where, and how. These can be tangible or intangible products and services, including your customer journey touchpoints and channels.

Your Insights Supply Chain

The Supply Chain Operations Reference (SCOR) model, developed by the Supply Chain Council, identifies five supply chain stages: Plan, Source, Make, Deliver, Return. We can borrow from this model to identify five critical stages for the insights supply chain.

1. **Focus on Supporting Your Business Strategy**. Michael Porter, one of the world's most influential thinkers on management and competitiveness, suggests your supply chain strategy defines the connection and combination of activities and functions throughout the value chain to fulfill the business value proposition to customers in a marketplace. Your company has a business strategy that hopefully leverages your organization's core competencies. These core competencies are what enable you to best differentiate your company from its competitors. Your strategy is your plan for how you win customer orders/deals and grow. Therefore, focus your supply chain on customer, market, and competitor insights that will most help you deliver on your strategy and value proposition. Prioritize your insights requirements based on your business strategy. Not sure where to start? As mentioned in Chapter 2, Gartner's *Customer Experience (CX) in Marketing Survey* suggests that companies are competing mostly or completely based on CX. This may be a good starting point for your strategy and insights requirements.

2. **Actively Design It.** Once you have alignment, the next step is to design an effective and efficient supply chain. You want to predefine how you'll move the materials and products through the stages of fulfillment. For our purposes, this work involves determining how you'll obtain the raw materials (data), how you'll convert it into insights, and how you'll distribute these insights and the associated recommendations to the rest of the network. Most likely you have some method of converting data into insights; therefore, the first step is to map and review how you do it today. Using the map, you can identify opportunities to improve the process. We often find this task is well-suited for a working session. As part of this process, explore ways to reduce costs, such as the cost of acquiring or managing data; reduce rework, such as having to redo analysis because the requirements were unclear; and improve accuracy.

3. **Optimize Insights-to-Action Performance**. It's one thing to produce the insights and quite another to deploy them. The performance of your insights supply chain should be measured against how well the insights are used to produce business success. The primary purpose of your insights supply chain is to produce business success and drive profitable growth, which comes from customers. Optimize and measure how well the insights are deployed and how these insights positively impact critical business measures, such as customer acquisition, win rates, customer loyalty, product adoption, cost to serve, and reduction in customer service issues. If you begin to see declines in these types of measures, add your insights supply chain into your root cause analysis to help you identify additional data or analytics that will help you "right the ship." If the supply chain is not producing actionable insights or not producing them fast enough, re-evaluate the chain and its components, starting with the requirements and

data. Make sure someone owns how the "insight-to-action" translation will be communicated and executed to all departments involved.

4. **Manage Its Suppliers**. All supply chains are only as strong as their weakest link. Some of the links in your insights supply chain may not be within your control, such as data from third parties or channel partners. Use supply chain management best practices with your data and tools partners. Have a plan to address supply chain bottlenecks (data shortages or delays) and increasing costs (tools and technology) to avoid having your insights supply chain disrupt business performance.

5. **Manage Your Data.** Your ability to deliver insights is only as good as your data. The quality of your data significantly impacts the quality of your insights. Therefore, the need to manage your data is paramount. Develop and rigorously employ a data management plan that should outline how you'll acquire, organize, inventory, and analyze the data as well as maintain its quality. Include your data policy in your data management plan.

These five critical stages in your insights supply chain, along with having the skills to do the work, are integral to your organization's growth. If you've got these five points covered, you're in good shape. If not, we strongly encourage you to invest the time necessary to do so.

Supply chains, including your insights supply chain, are the foundation for your company's value chain and critical to successfully compete. The more proactive you are about managing your insights supply chain, the greater your opportunity to maximize customer value and sustain a competitive advantage.

Gathering and Using Data

To achieve growth, your company, especially the Marketing function, needs to understand how to effectively use data to support upstream decisions as well as sync your content to your customer's buying process. While a great deal of data can be captured from digital platforms, marketing automation systems, customer relationship management systems, and other technologies, you still must reach out and connect directly with customers to gather competitive market intelligence.

Four foundational customer-focused initiatives that support this type of intelligence are:

1. Customer and technical advisory boards
2. Market and customer segmentation
3. Persona development
4. Customer journey and experience mapping

Many of these efforts take good-old-fashioned market research, which may take the form of surveys, focus groups, panels, and in-depth interviews conducted in person or virtually. Entire books have been devoted to conducting qualitative and quantitative research. If you're new to research methods, pick up a book and/or take a class. Research is fundamental to developing insights that become recommendations for growth, because it enables you to:

- Ask the questions you want to ask
- Begin with and test a hypothesis
- Sample to test for results that are valid and reliable
- Predict what might happen in the future

Once data is captured and organized, growth depends on being able to analyze the data to address at least four key questions:

1. What are our best segments/categories and product opportunities for growth for today and tomorrow?
2. Which existing and potential customers do we need to engage and how do we motivate them to engage?
3. What materials and assets, such as content, messaging, and positioning, should be brought into play?
4. How and when should these assets be distributed and through which channels, influencers, and partners?

The Value of Competitive Intelligence

I hope you concur that it's vital to conduct research that helps you learn more about your customers and market. If you're in a competitive market, and most of us are, it's just as critical to gather competitive intelligence (CI). CI analysis provides insight into marketplace dynamics and challenges in a structured, disciplined method to inform your business strategy. CI enables you to develop counter moves, plan for future customer and market opportunities, benchmark your organization, and assess the effectiveness of your positioning and messaging.

The first step of any CI is to determine what you need to know. Be clear about what you want to validate as well as learn about your competitors. For example, maybe you're trying to determine the unmet needs of your competitors' customers to motivate these companies to switch. It's very likely you already know some facts about the competition; make a list of what you think you know (for validation), and then a list of what you need to learn.

Research is only valuable if it is actionable. Frame the research in a way that will help you make business decisions. For example, should you pursue a market fraught with competition? If so, what's your strategy? Perhaps there's a need out there you've noticed that requires a whole new solution. If so, what are the customer specifications that will enable you to successfully compete? Acquire data that will help you assess your customer's requirements, buying criteria, and supplier preferences; market trends; and your competitors' capabilities and vulnerabilities.

Determine how you'll collect the data. There are a variety of ways to acquire customer and competitive intelligence. Is there valid secondary research available to fill the gaps? Can you harvest data from combing customer and competitor websites, company reports, online community discussions, customer reviews, analyst market reports, trade show material, and other information in the public domain? If these options don't yield what you need to know, you need to determine the best approach for conducting primary research—which requires determining the methodology, deciding on the study participants, creating the instrument, fielding the study, data coding and analysis, synthesizing the findings into actionable insights, and crafting the final report/presentation. It's a science and an investment.

Using Analytics

Decide and implement. Remember, the purpose of your research is to help guide your decisions and facilitate your success. Use the study findings to take action. Armed with the data, deriving insights to make appropriate customer, market, and product decisions will often require the application of analytics. Tom Davenport and Jeanne Harris, in their classic book, *Competing on Analytics: The New Science of Winning*, introduced business leaders to analytics and explored how analytics is rewriting the rules of competition. They provided a roadmap for becoming an analytical competitor and how to use analytics to create value and growth, which fall within the purview of Marketing.

There are two important ways organizations can use analytics to create growth opportunities. First is to identify high-value customers, i.e., customers who buy more of your current products, are most likely to buy your new products, and cost less to acquire and serve. Second is to identify the best programs and channels to engage, acquire, and retain these types of valuable customers.

Employing analytics takes expertise and time. It's a worthwhile investment, however, because it's the only way to gain the actionable insights you need to affect customers' brand preference, product adoption, and share of wallet, which in turn impacts market traction, penetration, and growth. The number of potential analytics projects is nearly as vast as the amount of data.

Analytics is hard and time-consuming, so finding a way to prioritize is important. One approach is to evaluate analytical projects against two criteria: ease of execution from easy to hard and value derived from low to high. By scoring each project by its value and ease-to-execute, you can organize projects into four categories.

- High-Value/Easy-to-Execute — Must Dos
- Low-Value/Easy-to-Execute — Quick Hits (things you can do in thirty days or less)
- High-Value/Hard-to-Execute — Transformative
- Low-Value/Hard-to-Execute — Nice to Have

We recommend to first focus on the high-value/easy-to-do as a way to demonstrate fast high-value wins. Then tackle the easy-to-execute/low-value for the next set of fast wins while you put a plan in place to address the hard-to-execute/high-value projects. This approach to the business takes skills and resources. If you don't have the analytics capabilities within Marketing, consider collaborating with folks internally or externally who do.

Introducing MarketingOps

To grow, companies must be able to meet increased demand. CEOs, CFOs, and COOs understand that operations management plays a key role in supporting the development, production, and delivery of products and/or services; it enables organizations to increase the level of performance to support scaling. Companies where Marketing has a strong emphasis on creating customer value are immersing themselves in data to make market, customer, and product/service decisions that create value for customers and shareholders.

The analytical approach we suggest takes skills and resources and it's not easy to scale. So, how do you scale it? We believe the optimal way is with Marketing Operations (MarketingOps), which is oxygen for growth. The role of MarketingOps has emerged and evolved due to the proliferation of marketing automation tools, increased pressure to prove the value of Marketing, and focus on connecting Marketing strategy with execution and actual results. A properly chartered and resourced MarketingOps function facilitates an agile Marketing organization.

MarketingOps helps set realistic expectation of performance and accountability. It ensures Marketing personnel know how to best use the processes, systems, and metrics. MarketingOps is the keeper of techniques, methods, activities, and processes essential to delivering a particularly superior outcome or result. As such, MarketingOps is responsible for the knowledge transfer, skills development, and benchmarking needed to sustain success. As the role has evolved, it has come to encompass the following five main responsibilities:

1. Defining and managing systems and tools
2. Developing and implementing metrics, infrastructure, and business processes

3. Establishing and communicating best practices
4. Managing the overall marketing budget and budgeting process
5. Identifying and deploying technology to support performance measurement and reporting

Marketing organizations with an effective MarketingOps function reap a number of essential benefits:

- Well-defined efficient and scalable processes, including data capture and management
- Analytics employed to identify and recommend value-based Marketing investments, including developing models to optimize channels
- Insights to facilitate strategic planning and growth
- Skills to develop models, such as ones addressing customer segmentation and attribution

Always Be Curious

This work is not optional any longer. It was with great pleasure that I recently had a chance to catch up with Becky Taylor. Becky and I came to Austin around the same time thirty-five years ago, and we both had careers at Motorola. Becky has been very much a part of the Austin startup scene, most recently as COO of SensorRx, a health-care software company focused on chronic disease management. In our conversation, Becky and I talked about organic growth, a shared passion that she described with her wise words, "You don't have a company if you're not growing. Every day is all about growth." Becky believes the key to growth is to "focus on getting the product right, getting the company right, and getting your sales right." This means you must be insatiably curious about what's going on in your market, with your customers, and with your competition.

This work is the only way to acquire the insights and intelligence needed to help uncover unmet customer needs, identify new markets, and predict what competitors are going to do. It can also help you stay abreast of trends and changes, and decide which growth opportunities to pursue and where to invest. Gathering insights and intelligence is not a one-time project; it should be an ongoing process. The competitive landscape, market, customer requirements, and trends continually change, so it's important to keep your customer insights and CI processes up-to-date.

TAKEAWAYS

- Your intuition may tell you that your business is wanted and needed, but it's nice to have data to back up that claim and provide directional guidance.
- Data comes in many forms and from many sources—from social media platforms, help and call centers, analyst and industry reports, your various internal systems (ERP, CRM, Marketing Automation Platforms, etc.), and intentional primary research. You need a process for gathering, analyzing, and deriving insights from data in any form from wherever it's stored.
- Traditional research is designed to test your hypothesis, your idea(s), and your assumptions—for example, assumptions about new product requirements, service priorities, buying and supplier preferences, and so on. It takes research to gain insight into these types of questions. Traditional market and customer research is ideal when you have customer-related questions to answer, such as why customers buy, how they buy, what they need to make a purchase decision, why they stay, why they leave, what they might need in the future.
- The more you can quantify how your solution will make a difference, the better.

TWENTY-THREE QUESTIONS TO PRIME THE GROWTH INSIGHTS PUMP

The purpose of gaining customer and market insights and delving into the competitive environment is to assess whether there's a market opportunity—a problem worth solving that you can solve. Most companies understand how to develop an opportunity. The real challenge is often generating good ideas in the first place. Most experts believe the generation of "good" opportunity ideas requires instituting a systematic process for vetting out possibilities.

Let's begin by establishing three criteria for what constitutes a "good" opportunity:

1. Fits with what you want to become as a company
2. Involves an attractive market
3. Takes advantage of a competitive opening

When you complete the Customer & Opportunity Insights phase of the wheel, you'll want to select a good opportunity that meets *all* three of these criteria. If you answer no to any of the questions that follow, focus on acquiring the necessary data to be able to change that to yes—to determine if you have an opportunity and it's worth pursuing.

	YES	NO
Are changes in the market or customer needs/preferences occurring?		
Do we know where in the supply chain disproportionate amounts of total profit are being made? Do we know how can we exploit these?		
Do we know what new markets can be served and/or what new products/services can be offered that fit our capabilities?		
Can we leverage our strategic core competencies to be a competitive advantage?		
Do we know which problems and markets leverage our strengths in management, technology, operations, marketing, distribution, and/or financing? Can we make changes to these capabilities to make it possible for us to pursue the opportunity?		
Can we leverage the markets where barriers and switching costs have real clout?		
Do we know the shortcomings of our and our competitors' current offerings, along with what improvements customers/markets want?		
Are we aware of what can we do to become more cost-competitive?		
Do we know what technology breakthroughs will address the most urgent—not biggest—customer problems and open a whole new market?		
Are we aware of what features and benefits can command a premium?		
Do we know what kinds of customers we fit particularly well—and what it would take to fit target customers better?		

	YES	NO
Do we know how can we achieve a higher share of wallet with existing key customers?		
Are there poorly served niches in existing markets that offer a competitive opening?		
Are there protected niches we can exploit and unique ways we can counter threats?		
Do we know where there is potential specialty status for us?		
Are we aware of who the weakest competitors are with businesses that are attractive to us?		
Have we identified what products/markets we should abandon?		
Do we know what markets are expected to have attractive growth rates and minimal downside threats?		
Do we know what markets are expected to have attractive future profit levels?		
Do we know in which products/markets we need to change our model or value proposition and what the will changes accomplish?		
Have we identified the markets where we're the price setter, and if we're leaving money on the table?		
Do we know what pricing innovations would improve profits?		
Do we know what opportunities might be created if we combined our intellectual assets with complementary suppliers/customers/competitors?		

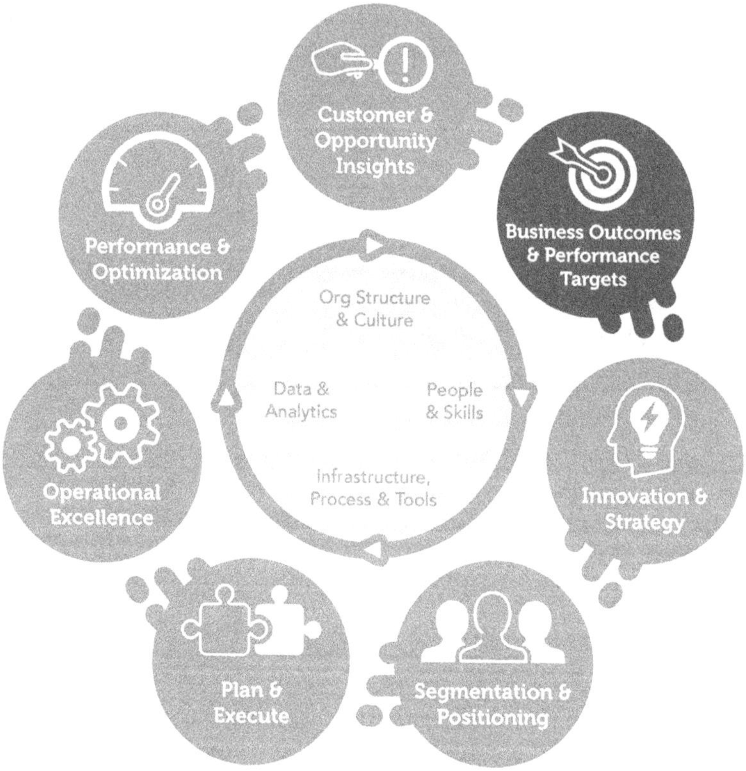
Customer & Opportunity Insights
Business Outcomes & Performance Targets
Innovation & Strategy
Segmentation & Positioning
Plan & Execute
Operational Excellence
Performance & Optimization
Org Structure & Culture
People & Skills
Infrastructure, Process & Tools
Data & Analytics

CHAPTER 4

BUSINESS OUTCOMES & PERFORMANCE TARGETS

DEFINING YOUR SUCCESS

"Today, nobody owns the customer. The customer owns you," were words written in 2005 by Jay Gailbraith, author of *Designing the Customer-Centric Organization: A Guide to Strategy, Structure, and Process*. He posits that customer-centric companies realize greater success than their product-centric colleagues. How are they different? Product-centric companies create products and then try to find customers for them—a shoe looking for a foot. Customer-centric companies, in stark contrast, create products that solve a customer problem—a shoe for a foot that stands for a twelve-hour shift.

This type of thinking—thinking centrically if you will—has numerous implications for a company. One of the most important implications is how it will define success. Certainly, every business needs to meet its financial targets. But how a company frames what it must do to achieve these targets reveals if it's embracing customer-centricity and primed to attain organic growth.

We refer to what the company must achieve to declare success as business outcomes, since an outcome specifies a result. Outcomes provide direction. Outcomes clarify success. Outcomes define priorities. Outcomes are all-inclusive. Every part of the organization should know the outcomes and its role in bringing them to reality.

The Need for Specific Goals

Many companies seem to have a problem expressing specific goals. You've probably heard goals like these:

- Our goal this year is to get closer to our customers.
- Next year's top priority is to launch our next-generation product.
- The most important business goal is to generate more new deals.

These goals, and goals like them, are so vague and ambiguous that they set many organizations up to fail. A good goal provides enough information and specificity that everyone knows what it must do to help the organization achieve the outcome and when the business can declare success.

Let's use the examples above to illustrate what we mean by unclear and vague, and how this situation can be improved.

Get closer to our customers. The first thing we need to understand is why this would be a goal. Is it a defensive or offensive goal? That is, is it a goal because your customers are at risk, perhaps vulnerable to competitive poaching due to a satisfaction issue or service quality? Or is it because you're taking a proactive approach and your company is focusing on growing the lifetime value of its customers? Also, which customers do you want to get closer to? All of them or some particular set? The answers to these questions are critical to establishing the outcomes; measures of success; and individual functions' objectives, strategies, and tactics. Imagine if the goal was restated as follows: "Our goal this year is to increase the top X percent customers' lifetime value by ensuring 100 percent retention and increasing the average number of products bought and used by this group from A to B." This goal statement is well-defined and your entire team now stands a better chance of success by developing metrics and objectives to impact lifetime value, tenure, and share-of-wallet.

Launch our next-generation product. The same process of discovery and clarification applies to this goal. Again, it's important to know if this is a defensive or offensive move. Are you coming in behind the competition and playing catch-up, or are you leading the way? The answer to this question will most likely impact your pricing and channel strategy. Is the go-to-market strategy for this product designed to tackle a new customer or market segment, or your existing customers? When is the optimum time to launch this product? For example, is it tied to a segment that relies on holiday sales? Specificity is required to really understand this goal. Imagine how the metrics, objectives, strategies, and tactics would be different if the outcome was written in one of these two but different ways:

1. Next year's top priority is to expand our market position in a new market segment for the company by launching our next-generation product by X date and securing three deals from three new OEM customers in the consumer electronics market segment.

2. Next year's top priority is to launch our next-generation product to maintain our foothold with our existing customers and ensure at least X percent of them trial the product by X date."

The outcomes are different as a result the metrics and objectives, and thereby the strategies and tactics will be different. In the first option, the key metrics will be around market share, rate of growth, new product acceptance, and new customer acquisition. In the second option, the primary metrics will be share-of-wallet, lifetime value, and new product acceptance. There are other options as well. Be specific and realistic about the situation and the Marketing team will know exactly what it has to do.

Generate more new deals. Marketing and Sales are two key internal partners often tasked with generating more deals. What's a new deal? Is it more business for existing customers or more deals from customers you've yet to acquire? Does size of the deal, margin, product/service purchased, or segment matter? Is the effort it takes to convert an opportunity to a deal of any consequence or are you willing to take any deal, anywhere, at any cost? Most companies aren't willing to do so, but the ambiguity can lead to reeling in bad business. When the goal is to generate more deals, it needs to be clear exactly what your company is really looking for and what constitutes a good deal. By now, we suspect you have the idea. So how might you rewrite this example of "generate more new deals" into something more specific and measurable?

Your Asset—The Customer Relationship

Customer-centric companies frame outcomes in terms of how they will create, retain, and grow profitable customer relationships. Per Gailbraith, the customer relationship is the asset. Your company doesn't market to buckets of revenue. Focusing on revenue is an internal point of view. As we've said and will continue to emphasize, customer-centric companies focus on what customers need and want, how to engage them, and how to create the best customer experience.

Phil Kotler, in his 1999 book, *Kotler on Marketing: How to Create, Win, and Dominate Markets*, provides the clues we need to establish business outcomes. He writes that a company must acquire, keep, and grow the value of profitable customers. Outcomes then need, in some way, to relate back to the answers to these two questions:

- How many net-new and/or additional dollars come from existing customers who have the problem we solve?
- How many of these customers do we want to serve?

Once you have those answers, you can begin to formulate how you'll serve customers better than the current options do—your competition or the status quo. If you've completed the work from the previous chapter, you should be armed with insights—information about the state and size of the target market, along with its needs and wants, and how your offer best meets them. Then you can develop strategies and programs designed to connect with these customers, increase and accelerate their consideration, and motivate their conversion to purchase. That's the focus of the next two chapters, which cover the weighty topics of innovation and strategy.

Do the Math

Your outcomes become the basis for your Key Performance Indicators (KPIs). These are the metrics your company is willing to invest in to change. Every function within your organization in some way must tie its work back to these KPIs and the outcomes they reflect. Each functional area in your organization must use the KPIs to establish its specific plan and associated performance targets that will enable the organization to achieve its outcomes. For example, let's say you need some number of net-new customers generating $X per transaction for a business unit by the end of the year. Before you can set a target for the number of customer deals, you'll need to know the typical sales cycle type, average deal size, typical conversion rate of opportunities to deals, and cost-to-acquire a net-new customer for this business unit.

This information can then be used to think beyond a revenue number and establish business outcomes by achieving the revenue target and associated measures of success, such as a target win rate number, the cost per new customer, and the actual number of customers acquired. With that back end of the equation, you can now work the front end and set a performance range to support the outcomes, such as how many customers/prospects a program must engage, and a target conversion rate and cost for them. We'll cover metrics further in the Performance & Optimization chapter.

The key point here is that growing the business means working the numbers, then tracking and reporting on the performance to the numbers. Taking a customer-centric view rather than an internally oriented revenue-centric view and "doing the math" facilitates the creation of an outcome that's relevant; has a measurable customer-focused value; and more importantly, positively impacts revenue and growth. With this said, take a moment to reflect on the goals, objectives, and targets in your current business, i.e., Marketing and Sales plans. Are these framed in customer terms or framed to achieve a certain amount of revenue for a product or region? Is the focus of the plan on counting revenue or counting and keeping customers? The more you can frame your outcomes around finding, keeping, and growing customers, the better.

What would that look like? Your statements would resemble these:

- Retain 90 percent of our top 20 percent of profitable customers
- Acquire fifty net-new customers with X problem from the Y industry and Z region
- Double the number of customers who have two or more products that enable us to grow in the category that solves X problem

Crafting these statements requires your organization to have the insights needed to understand the customer's problem, as well as:

- The magnitude of the problem
- The potential number of customers with the problem
- How many of these customers you currently serve

- How many potential customers you can acquire
- How your company's offers can solve this problem

Companies that think in terms of a portfolio of customers rather than a portfolio of products or brands will have outcomes that reflect this mindset.

All Hands on Deck

Once the outcomes are established, they become the mission for the organization. Every part of the organization is mobilized to achieve these outcomes, from Marketing to Sales, Product Development to Customer Service/Support, and Operations to Finance. All the functional department plans start with the same outcomes. The customer portfolio serves as the focal point for organizational conversations, priorities, decisions, and investment.

While this chapter is brief, establishing the outcomes and measures of success is one of the most important, challenging, and often overlooked steps in the wheel. With well-defined business outcomes, you can establish meaningful strategic metrics and specific and measurable objectives. These are the key elements for accelerating growth, creating customer value, and improving performance.

TAKEAWAYS

- Avoid vague goals. Invest in framing your outcomes and defining your measures of success. These serve as the beacon for everyone in the organization.
- Customer-centric companies establish outcomes and measures that focus on what customers need and want, how to engage them, and how to create the best customer experience.
- Every function within your organization in some way must tie its work back to your KPIs and the outcomes they reflect.
- Growing the business means working the numbers, then tracking and reporting on the performance to the numbers.

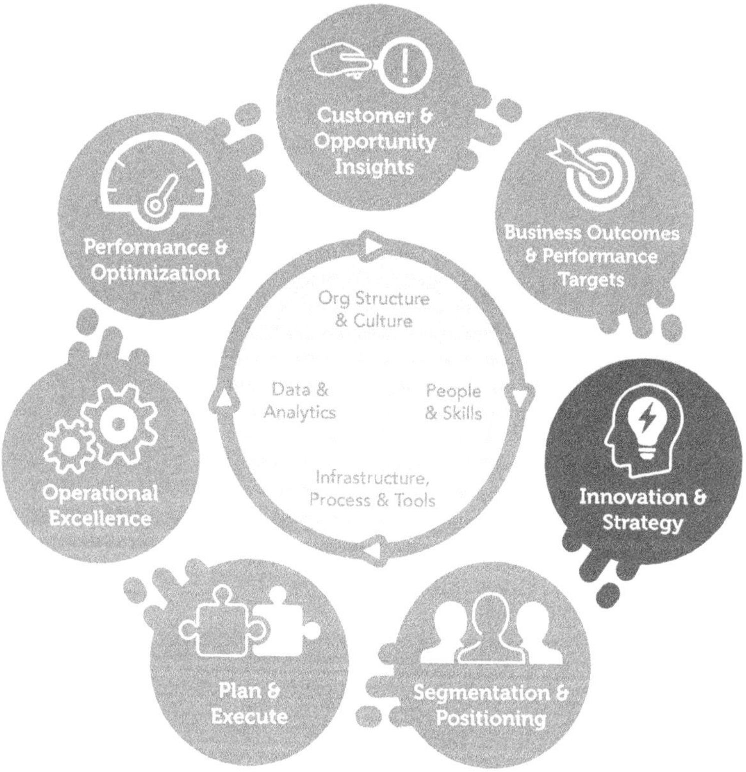

Customer &
Opportunity
Insights
Business Outcomes
& Performance
Targets
Innovation &
Strategy
Segmentation &
Positioning
Plan &
Execute
Operational
Excellence
Performance &
Optimization
Org Structure
& Culture
People
& Skills
Infrastructure,
Process & Tools
Data &
Analytics

CHAPTER 5

INNOVATION & STRATEGY—PART 1

STRATEGIZING TO SET THE STAGE FOR YOUR GROWTH

There's so much to the Innovation & Strategy part of the wheel that we decided to carve it up into two chapters; this one focuses on strategies that support organic growth, while Chapter 6 dives into the innovation process.

You've identified a problem faced by a market and/or your customers and it's big enough to warrant developing a solution. You believe you have a solution to solve the problem and have formed a company or practice. How do you grow? A conversation with Ziggy Shanklin, CEO of White Cloud Security, provides an excellent way to explore this question. "You need to have a strategy that not only helps you grow, but also reserves a channel for your future growth," he says. "When it comes to organic growth, you have to be thinking ahead. You can't just plan for trying to make your sales now. You have to be thinking about where am I gonna be five years from now?"[21] What does Ziggy recommend? His advice is to start looking at the market differently. This is the realm of strategy—looking at the situation in a different way to solve a problem or come up with a new approach. And do remember that whatever strategy you select needs to support your customer-centric outcomes.

Members of the C-Suite recognize the value of developing and executing a strategy to accelerate growth and improve performance. A CMO Council and Deloitte study[22] found that 70 percent of CEOs expect CMOs to lead the growth effort. Yet according to the study, just one in six of the 200 participating CMOs reported spending a lot of time teaming with leadership executives on global business and strategy. In a late 2017 *Forbes* article,[23] Leah Pope wrote about the immense pressure CMOs and Marketing face to drive and deliver measurable business growth. We're not seeing this abate among our customers, as we hear their boards reiterate their expectation for Marketing to lead the business forward.

A Marketing leader not participating in the conversation about strategy will not be able to assist the organization in its pursuit of growth. And, there are a couple things about growth that Marketing, and indeed everyone in the organization, must understand.

1. **Growth is a result of more than just selling**. You'll need to think beyond the pipeline to create the desired future state. The future is on its way. It will arrive tomorrow. None of us have crystal balls. The words of the Greek philosopher Heraclitus remain true: "All is flux, nothing is stationary." Change is inevitable. Technological advances, demographic shifts, mergers, and globalization cause change and affect the future. This means businesses must constantly be exploring how to build and grow a productive and profitable enterprise. Regardless of whether you think of the future as tomorrow or some longer time horizon, ideally you have a vision for the future state of your company. The key question is whether you have a strategy to achieve it.

2. **Growth decisions require understanding which customers, markets, and products to pursue and which ones to abandon**. I hope, if you're following the wheel, you've addressed this statement. If not, stop now and take the time to conduct the

research you need to gain knowledge about customer preferences, buying criteria, and the buying process. Implementing customer-centric growth strategies requires creating compelling messaging and content that resonates with and engages customers and prospects. These decision outputs require good data. To lead the charge, marketers must leverage analytics to capture the actionable insights needed to formulate the appropriate strategy.

Why Strategy?

Strategy is fundamental to the success and sustainability of all organizations. Per Michael Porter, the influential thinker introduced in Chapter 3, it's a matter of working out your company's best position relative not just to pricing pressures from rivals—do what everyone else is doing but spend less money doing it—or do something no one else can do. The latter approach requires you to consider how to create a new market (think blue ocean strategy), reinvent your business model, or find growth outside your core (such as entering an adjacent market). Gaebler.com, a news and information website that provides numerous resources for entrepreneurs, suggests that good business strategy should inspire company expansion and enable you to explore business opportunities outside of your standard business practice.

Organizations develop strategies designed to protect and/or gain market share and identify the opportunities that will yield the greatest return. Formulation of your strategy requires you to be acutely aware of and prepared for changing customer needs and potential shifts in your market. Before we discuss strategies in greater detail, let's briefly cover the topics of market validation, traction, penetration, and domination.

The best way to understand market validation is with the simple concept of proof. Validation implies that you have proved there is a market with a problem and you have a solution the market will adopt. At the other end of the spectrum is domination, where you control and influence the market. You're what people sometimes refer to as the "800-pound gorilla," an idiom for conveying that your company is the unbeatable player in the market. Validation is a long way from domination, and there are two major stops along the way: traction and penetration. Traction is the ability to hold your grip on the ground without sliding or slipping so you can move forward. Market traction is essential to building momentum, and as you gain it, the goal is to become a significant enough force in the market to penetrate the market and attain a market position in the category. It may be necessary to adjust your strategy, offer, messaging, channels, etc. along your path from validation to domination.

Options for Growth

To take advantage of the classic market strategies published by Igor Ansoff in his article "Strategies for Diversification" in the *Harvard Business Review* in 1957,[24] you'll need to have at least achieved validation. His model, known as Ansoff's Matrix, has been used for decades by organizations worldwide to address growth. The model presents four main options for growth:

1. **Market Penetration.** Focuses on increasing revenue by marketing and selling existing solutions to existing customers. You must already have validation and gained traction to leverage this strategy.

2. **Product Development.** Relies on replacing existing products with innovative solutions that are marketed and sold to existing customers. You must have at least achieved market penetration for this strategy to be successful.

3. **Market Development.** Achieves growth by taking existing products into a new market. This strategy is best achieved when you have validation, traction, and penetration in at least one market.

4. **Diversification.** An attempt to introduce new products in new markets where you may or may not have previous industry or market experience—which is extraordinarily risky. Ideally, you'll have a strong track record for validation, traction, penetration, and domination in a previous industry or market with an existing product or offer.

We've found the first three options are the best starting points for most companies, regardless of size or maturity, so let's dive a little deeper into them.

Market Penetration. Most experts support the premise that it's more cost-effective to keep a customer than to replace one. However, growth through existing customers and markets requires an increased focus on customer retention and identifying profitable growth opportunities for your core business. To create the strategy, your organization needs to measure and benchmark the current rate of revenue growth, market share, and customer experience for each of the core businesses. Marketing should know who are, and who are not, core customers; the firm's competitive differentiators; and where attractive growth opportunities exist to create high-impact, compelling value propositions for existing customers. This includes creating sub-segments, understanding buying patterns as well as revenue and profit contributions, and conducting A/B value proposition testing. Once again, you can see the importance of data and analytics.

You can only succeed with this strategy if you can retain your customers. Aim for at least 90 percent customer retention, a level that requires companies target and grow customers who will have the greatest life-time value and strategic fit. If you have customers, this is the first area in which to invest in your growth. The experience you deliver affects your customer retention, customer loyalty, and customer referral rates. Therefore, your post-sale processes are critical for this strategy.

Without retention, loyalty, and referrals, you can't leverage the second part of this growth strategy: winning new customers in this same market. You acquired your first customers, retained them, and they're buying more from you. It's also important that you can attract new customers. Doing so with your existing solutions demonstrates your ability to develop the market and grow your market share.

Product Development. Once you can retain your customers, you can identify where you can grow share-of-wallet or share-of-customer (i.e., footprint expansion). Keeping your customers is one thing; growing their value is another. Customer share is about how much your customers are investing in your products/services/solutions. It's a very strong indicator of brand preference. Customer share also reflects the depth of loyalty. It has implications for how quickly your new products will gain traction in the marketplace and your organization's overall customer lifetime value.

As you might expect, share-of-wallet is a powerful metric. It serves as a leading indicator as well as an indicator of performance relative to the competition. If your share-of-wallet is increasing, what customers are spending with competitors is by definition decreasing.

The second part of this growth strategy requires you to invest in services and products that enable you to grow the share a customer spends on the category with you. Developing new solutions is a major investment. About 80 percent of new products fail to generate a return to shareholders. Transitions to new products/services can be challenging, even upsetting to existing customers. Anticipate resistance and develop a plan to secure their support. To improve the success rate of new products and succeed with this strategy, integrate your customers into the development process. Customer Advisory Boards, for example, can serve as an excellent vehicle to support this process. Focus on making sure prospects/customers see how the new solutions offer a new benefit that's seen as unique.

With new products, timing is paramount. Your new solutions must come to the market at the right time for the buyers. We can all recall products that were too soon to market. In 1992, AT&T brought a videophone to market.[25] That's right, a videophone, a precursor to FaceTime and other products like it on the market today. It was a terrific product, and a perfect illustration of a product-centric approach: a shoe looking for a foot. Another example of the pitfall of product-centricity is Living.com, an online furnishings site and precursor to sites such as Wayfair and Overstock. Living.com launched in 1999 and was deceased by 2000.[26] I remember sitting in the meeting room the day the company announced the launch, and hearing some of the questions posed—which made it clear the company had skipped the chapters on insights and intelligence and customer-centric outcomes. No doubt you can think of other product-centric first movers that failed.

Your new solutions must also in some way enable you to create a barrier to entry for competitors. Research by Peter Golder and Gerard Tellis[27] found almost half of the market pioneers (first movers) in their sample of 500 brands in fifty categories failed. Their study suggested that fast followers (early market leaders) experience greater long-term success. Again, we can think about first movers—companies that were first with a new idea or product—who faced fierce competition because the barrier to entry was minimal. Uber and Lyft, both early market leaders of rideshare platforms, illustrate this idea.

A new solution that isn't properly supported by Marketing is doomed. Whatever you invested in developing the product, you'll need at least that level of investment to launch and market it. Much has been written on commercializing innovation and we'll touch on this more in the next chapter.

Market Development. This approach isn't so much about creating a new market, which is hard and expensive, but about moving into markets that are new to you. One option is using an adjacency strategy, which can often help pave the way to a new market. Entering adjacent markets that have strong, strategic links to your core business and mirror your customers and their problem is a viable approach. This strategy becomes especially important when you've reached maximum share/growth in your core business. Typically, the easiest route to adjacent markets is with proven products and/or services. This strategy, like any, requires new market data—potential customer segmentation and their buying process, along with the analytics to help you score and determine the best segments and markets to pursue.

When we work with customers seeking growth, we use the adjacency approach as presented by Chris Zook of Bain & Company in his book, *Profit from the Core, Growth Strategy in an Era of Turbulence*. His approach is based on the fundamental premise that successful market strategies start with protecting the core business through seeking growth in core business adjacencies. Through adjacency expansion, your organization moves into related segments or businesses that use, and usually reinforce, the strength of your profitable core.

The approach we use encompasses the following broad steps:

1. Define all the dimensions of doing business in markets related to your core business.

2. Map possible growth opportunities as you move outward from the core in each dimension, e.g., new geographies, channels, products, and customers.

3. Assess and choose the right adjacencies.

The crucial step is to identify potentially viable adjacent market opportunities, starting with the following process:

- Examine the adjacent markets you're already serving to evaluate how well you're doing in terms of revenue, market share, and profitability.
- List adjacencies your organization has previously considered or rejected and determine if the reasons for the decision are still relevant.
- Identify other existing adjacencies you know of that would require two or more strategic moves, such as addressing or creating a competitive advantage related to quality, innovation, or customer experience, or adjacencies competitors are pursuing.
- Consider what potential adjacencies might emerge due to a technology advancement, or other market or economic developments.

After completing this process, it's very possible you'll have a long list of possibilities. We've found a screening process is necessary to narrow the list, and suggest answering the questions below as part of developing your strategy and preparing to enter a new market:

1. What is your objective in entering the new market? Have an explicit objective and a defined revenue and time frame target. If you can't articulate an explicit objective and aren't able to set revenue and time frame targets, wait to enter until you can. Manage your timeline. Entering and expanding into a new market takes time. The sales cycle will probably be longer because you don't have the credibility and experience. After you do your initial sales forecast and timeline, lower it. Evaluate the market's attractiveness based on the assumption that it will take twice as long as you think it will. If it takes longer than expected to reach the revenue target, can you stick it out?

2. Why can't you achieve this objective in your existing market? Breaking into a new market is hard work. It takes a large

investment. It's generally easier to sell into a market that knows you and your products, one where you have references and an established reputation and track record. Use this question as a gate. If you can achieve the objective by staying in your existing market, reconsider entering a new market.

3. Do you have a plan and the resources? Make a detailed rollout plan and identify the important milestones and challenges. Don't take any action until you have a plan with contingencies. Having a plan is one thing; being able to implement it is another. Verify you have the resources, and a product and corresponding value proposition for it for a new market.

4. Do you know who and what you're up against? Every market has its incumbent competitors. Before you enter a new market, be certain you know who you'll face, how they sell, and why they win.

5. What's your plan to sustain your efforts in your current market? Pursuing a new market may mean you take your eye off the ball. Assume at the start that the pursuit of a new market will affect your existing resources as well as your existing market and revenue from it, and plan accordingly. Be sure you have a plan for reassuring your existing customers that they're still important.

While many market strategists generally agree that factors such as timing, scale relative to the competition, and the ability to leverage complementary assets are the keys to successful market entry, most experts believe that for every successful market entry, about four fail. One of the biggest reasons for failure is relying too heavily on an inside view. All too often, executives believe a company's skills are more relevant than they truly are, or the potential market is bigger than it really is. An inside view may not provide enough insights into how competitors will respond. The costs of miscalculation can be extensive. Taking an outside view can help you develop objective predictors of success.

Do Your Recon

Reconnaissance (recon) is a very important concept, especially regarding entering a new market; before barreling in, learn everything you can. As part of your recon and before you take up the chase, there are five questions you should answer to come up with a viable plan (and budget) for going after a new market, in the following order:

1. Start with the Whos. "Who" means to what market, subsegments, companies, and personas will you be marketing? Who is the competition and how do they go to market? Who is knowing the influencers, e.g., analysts, consulting companies, and publications. And, who else will need to be involved in the complete solution, e.g., an integration or distribution partner?

2. Answer the Whys. "Why" specifically does the market need your proposed product, your service, your company? Why now?

3. Crystalize the Whats. "What" do you provide that answers the "why" differently from solutions already being marketed? What are the buying criteria and preferences? What is your value proposition and promise?

4. Develop the Hows. "How" do prospects want you to connect with and engage with them? Think Customer Journey Mapping. How will you engage influencers? How do you develop new partnerships or extend existing ones? How will you engage, provision, and train internal departments and external partners to sell and support the new solution in the new market?

5. Determine the When. Is there a seasonality to the solution? Is there a major industry event such as a trade show that would be a good time to launch with the press, analysts, and customers?

When you know the answers to these questions, ideally in the above-listed order, you're ready to create and implement your Marketing plan and supporting budget request.

Even if you don't have the resources to conduct primary research, you can use these five affordable ways to come up the learning curve:

1. Read all the publications—online and offline—that cover the market.

2. Attend as many industry trade shows and conferences as you can over a nine- to twelve-month period.

3. Contact other companies you do business with. They may already be in this market and able to provide some insight.

4. Consider hiring an industry expert to serve as a consultant or join your board.

5. Explore being a subcontractor to a prime contractor in the market.

Understanding the industry will be paramount to your success. Look for ways to shorten your learning curve about a new market with the above suggestions. If you can't afford the cost of failure, consider investing in creating a reference class. (See "The Value of a Reference Class" on page 86.)

And, as you evaluate your options for a new market, make sure the ones you select meet all three of these criteria:

- Fits with who you want to become as a company
- Involves an attractive market
- Takes advantage of a competitive opening

Research from McKinsey[28] suggests that six factors predict a company's success with market entry success:

1. Entering at a minimum efficiency scale
2. The relationship of your current portfolio of products and services to the intended market
3. Strong complementary assets
4. Order of entry—such as first mover, fast follower, or laggard
5. Industry lifecycle stage
6. Degree of technological innovation

Remember, if you're going to leap into a new market, it's important that you understand the market, the requirements to serve that market, and how your offer creates value for the customers in that market. This means you're going to need to invest some time and money. It also often means different positioning, pricing, and promotion strategies to address the different needs, operating processes, and buying patterns in new markets.

The Business Ecosystem

Entering a new market means taking a chance. The more you understand the ecosystem in the market and how to participate in the ecosystem, the better your odds of success. The concept of an ecosystem comes from the fields of biology and ecology. It describes how living and nonliving entities such as plants, animals, microbes, air, water, and soil interact with each other. These communities that exist in nature can also be applied to business.

The concept of a business ecosystem first appeared in the May-June 1993 *Harvard Business Review* article, "Predators and Prey: A New

Ecology of Competition" by James Moore.[29] Moore defines a business ecosystem as, "An economic community supported by a foundation of interacting organizations and individuals—the organisms of the business world. The economic community produces goods and services of value to customers, who are themselves members of the ecosystem. The member organisms also include suppliers, lead producers, competitors, and other stakeholders. Over time, they coevolve their capabilities and roles and tend to align themselves with the directions set by one or more central companies. Those companies holding leadership roles may change over time, but the function of an ecosystem leader is valued by the community because it enables members to move toward shared visions to align their investments, and to find mutually supportive roles."

To be able to take advantage of an ecosystem or enter a new one you need a map. An ecosystem map provides a way for an organization to identify market and customer opportunities where they can expand and grow, what and who might thwart or help their efforts, and where they may be facing risk. This map or model serves as an excellent strategic tool. It helps you understand your position in the market (who and where competitors and potential partners are); keep tabs on what's happening in the market; and know where and with whom you should place your valuable resources, such as attention, energy, and money.

Now let's say you can't map the ecosystem or won't because it's quite difficult. Are you out of options? No; here are some other things you can do to minimize the risk of entering a new market:

- **Use Affiliates.** Affiliates are entities that send customers to you in exchange for a commission. A reason for using affiliates is that they may have a solid footing in a market you're trying to gain access to. Affiliates can earn as much as 15 percent of every purchase.

- **Mine Second and Third Tiers**. Second- and third-tier markets present solid new market opportunities and support answering the questions of "who" and "why." When researching these groups, look for cluster opportunities that might suggest an untapped market for your company. Your next new market could be hiding inside your own business.

- **Tackle A Niche.** A niche represents a small but profitable segment of a market suitable for your offer. One approach to entering into a niche is to partner with a company with complementary products/services in the targeted niche—a subset of a larger market that has its own needs or preferences that are typically different from the larger market. This can be a very cost-effective approach for small firms.

- **Partner.** Collaborate with a firm that's already well established in the ecosystem. For this to work, you'll need to bring something of value to the partnership. This could be a product line, service capabilities, or access to new customers.

Pace yourself to sustain growth and include these two areas on your growth roadmap:

- Routes-to-market, which are how you'll efficiently and effectively deliver your products/services to end-users. Will you be delivering these directly or leverage partners or a combination of these—such as providing a software platform that's implemented by a third party? What form will delivery take, e.g., are you reading this book or listening to it?

- New regions, including international markets

Focus on the Future

Regardless of the options you select, every good strategy that drives long-term growth and profit answers these two primary questions:

1. What is the envisioned future of your company?
2. How will you achieve this future?

The answers to these questions serve as the backdrop for your strategy and guide your choices regarding which opportunities to pursue and just as importantly, which not to pursue; which operations to develop, streamline, or jettison; and what skills your organization needs or will need. For most organizations, resources are finite. Your strategy dictates what resources, offers/services, operations, and capabilities are required to successfully compete. When well-formulated, your strategy is an engine for growth and defines your priorities. Without clarity of strategy, your team is at risk of aimlessly moving from one activity to another.

The following three steps are designed to help you begin to address these two questions.

Step 1: Assess and Synthesize. We're once again back at the starting point, the need for data. To complete this step, you may need to conduct primary and secondary research, because you'll want to account for the current state and emerging opportunities. To envision the future, several assessments are required:

- The current state of the world (what's happening on the world stage, i.e., stable, uncertain)
- The market (what's happening with your current market; is it growing, stagnating)
- Your competition (what they're doing, what's happening in your ecosystem; is it consolidating, expanding)

- Your customers (where are their pain points and what's working for them)
- Your company (where it is today)

Once you have a clear understanding of the current state, you can begin to explore emerging opportunities. Start by discussing questions such as: What lies on the horizon in terms of the world, market, competition, customers? What are some of the primary trends emerging in the world? What are some implications to the industry?

You're looking for trends that are relevant to your market, customers, and company. Some trends affecting your customers, for example, are (1) the increasing use of automation in manufacturing and automobiles; (2) the use of drone technology; (3) the growing role of artificial intelligence (AI); and (4) the implications of omnichannel financial services, retail, travel, and hospitality. These are just a few. As we've noted on several occasions, we live in a dynamic, ever-changing world.

Step 2: Envision and Decide. This step involves the process of examining how the trends you identified in the first step apply to and impact your customers and company. Take the time in this step to brainstorm around this question: What opportunities emerge based on the trends we've identified? Don't try to determine in this step how viable each opportunity is or whether you can take advantage of it.

After you complete the brainstorm step, establish criteria for how you'll evaluate each opportunity. For example, you may want to include criteria related to cost, potential market size, number of existing customers that could be initial adopters, and so on.

Choose a future. Remember, what you decide not to pursue *now* is just as important. That doesn't mean you must forgo it forever. Consider creating a "parking lot" or repository for these ideas and a plan to revisit them. At some point, the timing might be better for these opportunities.

Complete your evaluation process and determine what's possible and feasible. Use gap analysis—assessing actual performance against potential or desired performance—as part of your process, and then select one or two of the best scenarios. Commence scenario analysis before deciding on a future direction. (See "Creating Scenarios for Analysis" on page 88.)

Step 3: Take Action. You've made a choice. This third step is where the rubber meets the road. The potential future and the strategy you've selected can only be realized if you make and implement a plan.

Once you've selected your growth strategies, the next step is to give them life. A common output of your strategy is a strategic plan. Typically, a strategic plan outlines how the strategy will be deployed and specifies how desired results are expected to be achieved. These are often referred to as strategic initiatives. The strategic initiatives are the basis for your organization's business outcomes.

In the mid-1990s, Arthur Andersen conducted a survey that found companies with a written strategic plan had 63 percent higher revenue growth and 100 percent more profit than those companies without a plan. A more current study by The Alternative Board (TAB)[30] reported that three-quarters of the businesses surveyed believe a written strategic plan causes their business to perform at a higher level.

Craft your plan so it clarifies the vision and increases the alignment across the organization. Make it serve as the reference point for decision-making and the foundation for each of your functions' outcome-based measurable plans. We believe a strategic plan is one of the most valuable efforts and assets for every organization. Your strategic plan provides your roadmap to your future. It's about what you'll proactively do to create, deploy, and measure your success.

Measuring Success

Success must be more than a sales and/or revenue target. It's possible to achieve sales and revenue targets and still fail at the strategy. Be clear about how you'll measure the success of your strategy.

The opposite is true as well. It's possible for a strategy to be working but the sales numbers lagging. Without clear measures and metrics for how to measure the success of the strategy, your team is operating blindly. Some possible ways to measure strategic success include the rate of organic growth, increases in market share, and upticks in customer equity. We'll talk more about measures and metrics in Chapter 10, which is focused on performance and optimization.

Identify the key steps for how to realize the future. How well you understand the current situation, the true intent of the market, your ability to validate your assumptions, and your organization's competencies and vulnerabilities are all key factors that will determine how successful you are in developing a winning strategy. Keep in mind that your competitors may be going through the same process.

Once you identify how you'll measure the success of the strategy, you'll need to make sure each operational plan has a set of measurable objectives and activities tied directly to these metrics and performance targets. For Marketing, examples of metrics might be the share of preference and win rate. Then, it's a matter of creating a viable realistic plan that you can resource and execute. This is the focus of Chapter 8, which is dedicated to planning and executing.

Let's Be Clear

The business environment is fluid, with technological, social, and political change occurring with increased frequency. Successful businesses realize achieving growth while adapting to the rate of change and staying in tune with the market require staying strategically nimble. Customer insights, competitive intelligence, market research, and a clear understanding of your ecosystem enable you to do that and inform your strategy development. Armed with insights from your research, experience, and expertise in the market and with your customers, you can explore new ideas for your company that enable you to find, keep, and grow the value of your customers and maintain or increase your competitive advantage.

The bottom line: Having a clear growth strategy and strong execution are essential to achieving profitable growth. Marketing can be a major contributor to both strategy and its execution by driving innovation and leveraging actionable insights derived from data and analytics.

TAKEAWAYS

- Remember that whatever strategy you select needs to support your customer-centric outcomes.
- Formulation of your strategy requires you to be acutely aware of and prepared for changing customer needs and potential shifts in your market.
- With regard to strategizing for growth, market penetration, product development and market development are the best starting points for most companies, regardless of size or maturity.
- Two possible market development options are using an adjacency strategy or leveraging your business ecosystem.
- Your strategy dictates what resources, offers/services, operations, and capabilities are required to successfully compete. When well-formulated, your strategy is an engine for growth and defines your priorities.
- Be clear about how you'll measure the success of your strategy.

THE VALUE OF A REFERENCE CLASS

A reference class, which allows you to play the probabilities, is comprised of a set of companies that made similar decisions in the past to use as a reference point. This approach allows you to counteract the tendency of many decision-makers to fall into the "confirmation trap": seeking information that confirms their hypotheses. A reference class can also be used to estimate the size of a market. Estimating a market's potential size typically involves categorizing customers into several segments and then using pricing and elasticity assumptions to estimate the percentage of buyers in each category the company might capture.

Too often, companies are overly optimistic about initial market estimates regarding size and growth rate. Also, they often forget to include the lifecycle stage of the market in their calculation. Your reference class can be a useful way to improve estimates of market size by serving as a benchmark. You can use your reference class to set reasonable bounds on market share. If, for example, the reference class attained only a 3 to 5 percent market share, that may be an important data point in your decisions.

The broader your reference class, the more likely you'll have a realistic idea of the costs associated with attaining various market share levels. Cost estimates far below the realized costs of the reference class should make decision-makers think again.

What do you need to create a reference class? A broad reference class of at least five similar entry decisions in the past enables you to analyze more outcome possibilities—and more is better. This is a great way to leverage the experience of other companies and industries.

Here are a few tips for constructing and leveraging a reference class:

- Review what factors are most relevant for success.
- Identify and select entrants in other industries, involving as many of the most important factors as possible. It's important to uncover successful and failed entries so the reference class approximates the distribution of actual outcomes. The greater the overlap with the experience of the industry in question, the more valuable each example will be for the reference class. It can often be useful to reach out across different industries.
- Once you create the reference class, use it to identify the key determinants of successful market entry and answer these types of critical questions:
    - Which product attributes and business models have succeeded in the past?
    - How were the winners superior marketers?
    - What did they do to achieve outstanding distribution systems?

Because the costs and risk of market entry are high, creating a reference class is worth the effort. This approach allows you to combine inside and outside views to improve your odds of market entry success.

CREATING SCENARIOS FOR ANALYSIS

A scenario is defined as "a description of possible events." Scenarios are a powerful tool for understanding potential business situations, such as customer experience, and then developing appropriate strategies for each of them. The value of creating scenarios is that they allow you to consider a range of possible outcomes and drivers of change. When you can anticipate a problem, you can modify a business process before it occurs.

The great thing about scenario analysis is that you don't need anything more than your imagination. The goal is to create as many different combinations of potential events as you can conceive. Then, by analyzing each potential scenario, you can assess its likeliness to occur and decide what, if any, proactive action is necessary. For example, you learn your company may face an increased risk of customer defection should one or more of your analyzed scenarios occur.

Creating scenarios that will be useful in helping to make you more agile does require data and timing information. When gathering your data, use the following questions as a guide, along with adding specificity, depending on what aspect of your customer's experience you're addressing.

- What can change, and by how much?
- What data is predictive of a key prospect or customer behavior?
- What data is essential for effectively engaging with customers and prospects?
- What data is required to support a consistent cross-channel customer experience?

It might help to look at the past and think about what you wish you had known then that you know now. Identify the industry, political, economic, societal, technological, and legal trends that might affect those issues.

Proven Principles to Help Craft Your Scenarios

Creating scenarios is both art and science. Want to give it a try? Follow these ten steps to get started.

1. Define your scope to look for events that are certain or nearly certain to happen within a specific time frame. As much as possible, try to take a customer-centric view of the event from the perspective of customer experience, e.g., running out of a high-demand product or not having enough technical people to solve customer issues in a timely matter. We found this to be the case when we hit a home run with the introduction of the first 8-bit HCMOS microcontroller with onboard electrically erasable memory. As the potential applications for the product exploded, we ran out of capacity, forcing us to allocate the product across the customer base. Few, if any, customers received all the product they purchased. Yet, these customers had ramped up their facilities in anticipation of receiving the product to support their customer demand.
2. Generate scenarios that cover a broad range of outcomes. Again, think in terms of customer outcomes, e.g., customers terminating contracts or delaying renewals of a software subscription service. Several scenarios might have the same outcome, so you may want to organize these into themes.
3. Identify at least three driving factors and associated critical uncertainties. A driving factor in customer experience over the years has been technology—from call centers and automated voice response to self-service

via the website. AI is an emerging technology that may impact customer service. Technology is fraught with uncertainties, such as pricing, implementation, and adoption.

4. Develop at least four scenarios to address each of these uncertainties. (Why four? To avoid leaning toward the middle one.)
5. Evaluate each scenario in terms of its likelihood within the time frame. Place scenarios outside the time frame in the "parking lots" to address later. Be careful not to discard scenarios that initially seem too far outside the box. These can provide valuable insights and potential risks. Sometimes the most interesting and insightful scenarios are the ones that at first seem the most unlikely.
6. Make a weighting scale to evaluate the probability and risk of each scenario. (Many organizations have limited resources, so prioritize them if addressing every scenario isn't possible.)
7. Conduct research to flesh out the details and increase your understanding of each potential scenario. Evaluate each scenario based on the research findings.
8. Select the scenarios where the outcome seems most likely.
9. Consider what processes, skills, or systems will be affected and what resources are needed to offset or prepare for each scenario.
10. Produce and implement action plans to address each of the scenarios.

Securing a Solid Plan for Scenario Analysis

Creating and analyzing scenarios is far more than an exercise of your imagination. Scenarios help you understand the magnitude of a trend and the uncertainty of your environment. They provide a vehicle for developing a set of strategies that optimize your chances of success under nearly all possible outcomes. It's an excellent approach for anticipating and addressing customer experience pitfalls.

THE HISTORY OF ANALYTICS

The focus on data and analytics is not new. As we mentioned in Chapter 2, they're primary components of the axle subsystem and serve as the driveshaft for the Circle of Traction. The driveshaft is what creates torque—the force that produces the rotation. Analytics enable you to make data-derived decisions.

For decades, organizations have been seeking ways to make better informed business decisions and optimize performance. The figure below shows this evolution of analytics from the 1980s to today.

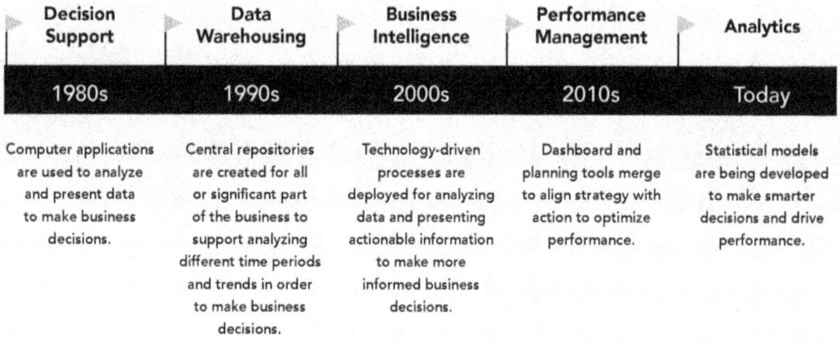

Figure 2: The History of Analytics. Source VisionEdge Marketing.

Early on, the focus was on data acquisition—what data, how to acquire it, where to keep it. Armed with data, the next step was learning how to use it to make decisions. Some organizations are still in these early stages; others have moved on to using data to optimize performance. Best-in-class organizations are now exploring how to use data to drive processes and predict trends and behavior patterns, improving their ability to serve their customers, grow, and compete. Thomas H. Davenport and Jeanne G. Harris, who wrote *Competing on Analytics: The New Science of Winning*, found that organizations using complex analysis and making data-intensive decisions are successfully changing the way they manage themselves and compete in the marketplace.

The exponential increase in data over the last few decades has had a significant impact on the evolution and adoption of analytics. Per the IDC,[31] the digital universe is doubling every two years and will reach 40,000 exabytes (40 trillion gigabytes) by 2020. Without advanced analytics, including machine learning algorithms, it will be impossible to discover and communicate meaningful patterns in all this data to extract the business insights needed to drive more effective business decisions.

Often, the biggest hurdle for organizations is being able to unlock value from data by analyzing and acting on it. As explained by Hal Varian, Google's chief economist,[32] data is widely available; what's scarce is the ability to extract wisdom from it. In a world deluged with data, our real task isn't to focus on more data, but rather to focus on capturing the right data and then analyze it in a way that gives us the power to see (knowledge) and act (wisdom). Hence, the importance of analytics—"the systematic analysis of data"—to discover, interpret, and communicate germane patterns in data. Analytics are the foundation of fact-based decision-making.

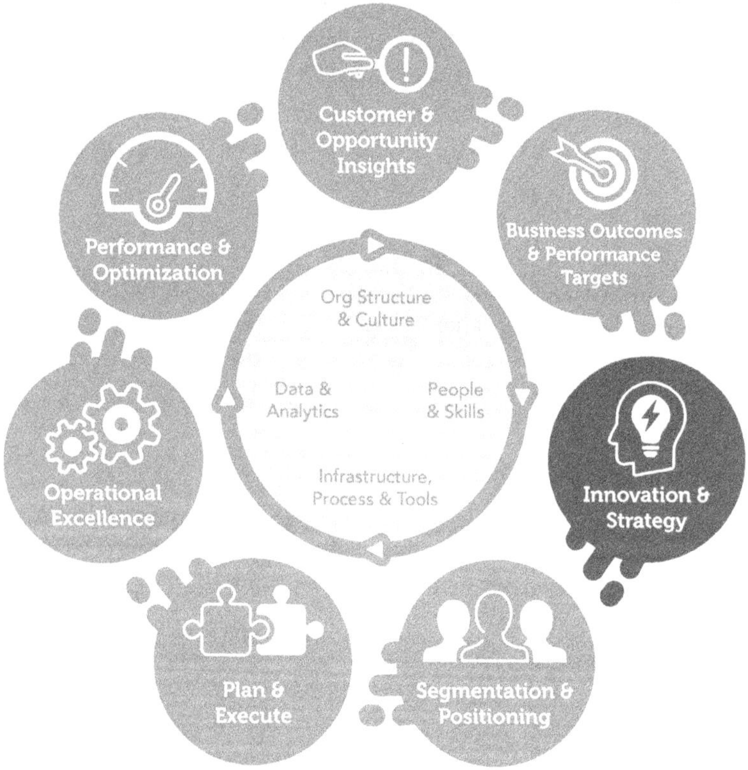

Customer & Opportunity Insights
Business Outcomes & Performance Targets
Innovation & Strategy
Segmentation & Positioning
Plan & Execute
Operational Excellence
Performance & Optimization
Org Structure & Culture
People & Skills
Infrastructure, Process & Tools
Data & Analytics

CHAPTER 6

INNOVATION & STRATEGY—PART 2

ATTAINING ORGANIC GROWTH THROUGH INNOVATION

In Chapter 5, we explored a number of strategies to enable you to attain organic growth with existing products. Strategies to expand using existing products are generally easier because the product have market validation. You may recall that in the Ansoff Matrix, there are strategies associated with bringing new solutions to existing or new markets. These strategies are for the purpose of expanding your footprint within your customer base/market segment, or to expand into new markets. They are more challenging because innovation is hard and fraught with risk.

Innovation can take the form of completely new or an enhancement and be associated with a product, service, or process; all are designed to improve customer experience and engagement, differentiate your offers from the competition, and enhance your competitive advantage. As such, innovation takes a process, which is the focus of this chapter. You may be thinking, wow, we're halfway through the book and we're just now talking about innovation. Many people might put innovation and differentiation at the very start. Certainly, product-centric companies think this way. The adage, "if we build it, they will come" applies to this notion. Forrester refers to today's business customer-centric environment as the Age of the Customer.[33]

Customer-centric innovation and differentiation are required to gain market momentum and accelerate product adoption. Companies and their boards and shareholders are impatient, often unwilling to wait for new products to cross the chasm. For more about this, check out Geoffrey Moore's work, *Crossing the Chasm: Marketing and Selling High-Tech Products to Mainstream Customers.* Bringing customer-centric solutions is the only way for a new solution to move rapidly from validation and traction to penetration and hopefully domination in a category. Over the next three years, to generate organic growth, more than half the companies participating in a recent McKinsey study[34] indicated that the creation of new products, services, or business models will be a key to their strategy.

Introducing Something New

Today, there is a great deal of focus on innovation being disruptive. That is when an innovation creates a new market and business model that result in established players failing. Uber and Lyft are often used to illustrate this idea. If you step back, though, you can see that Uber and Lyft took an established idea of an online marketplace (eBay was founded in 1995) that brings buyers and sellers together, and using a mobile platform, brought it to a new segment. While it certainly disrupted the traditional taxi industry, was that innovation?

Yes. Innovation is simply defined as the introduction of something new. It's the word *new* in reference to a solution that requires some exploration. New can be something that never existed before, like the first wheel, invented in 3500 B.C. in Mesopotamia for pottery. Three hundred years later, someone "got the idea" for a new use for the wheel—transportation—attaching wheels to chariots.[35] The word *chariot* comes from the Latin term *carrus.* Chariots used in military parades were called a car. In this example, an existing product was modified for a new purpose—also new and an innovation.

Speaking of cars, in 1885, Carl Benz introduced the first compact high-speed single-cylinder four-stroke engine installed horizontally at the rear, the tubular steel frame, the differential, and three wire-spoked wheels. Yes, this was the first automobile, or what he called in his patent, the first "vehicle powered by a gas engine." The wheel used in transportation integrated into a new type of vehicle that created a new product; it was a transformation of an established product in an established segment for a new market. The ability to attach wheels to conveyances and appliances transformed the transportation industry right along with the agriculture and shipping industries.

Henry Ford was right on the heels of Benz, building his first automobile in 1896. It was Ford who sixteen years later in 1910 innovated automobile manufacturing with the concept of the assembly line.[36] It wasn't, however, until 1955, seventy years later, that automobiles became mainstream.[37] That's a long time in today's terms to wait for a new product to go from conception to mainstream adoption. Along the way, Charles Goodyear invented vulcanization, a process that made rubber waterproof and winterproof, while at the same time preserving its elasticity. John Dunlop took that innovation and produced the first practical pneumatic tire. Companies such as Goodyear, Michelin, and Continental continue to bring innovation to tires.[38] Let's not forget the original purpose of the wheel, the potter's wheel. The advent of the Industrial Revolution in the eighteenth century facilitated the innovation of the potter's wheel when mechanical power wheels began to be developed. The new mechanical/electrical power wheel made it possible for the potter's wheel to run at a continuous steady speed or varying speeds controlled by a foot pedal.

As you see, there's a lot of nuance to new and innovative. While a solution can be completely new, never having previously existed; new as a result of improvements; or merely new to your portfolio, sustainable organic growth requires the ability to be innovative. A survey by McKinsey & Company[39] found that 94 percent of managers are unhappy with their company's innovation. Many organizations have come to believe that to be successful the new solution must be disruptive. But as the story of the wheel reveals, disruption is not synonymous with innovation. Research by W. Chan Kim and Renée Mauborgne, professors of strategy at INSEAD and codirectors of the INSEAD Blue Ocean Strategy Institute who wrote *The New York Times* and *Wall Street Journal* bestseller, *Blue Ocean Shift: Beyond Competing* and the global bestseller *Blue Ocean Strategy*, concludes it's possible to be innovative without being disruptive. It's less about disruption and more about creating a product that will be embraced and adopted by the market.

The Product-Market Fit

New in business is only valuable if it leads to customers. This is why Dave Sikora, longtime Austin software industry veteran and experienced CEO, claims organic growth "comes down to product-market fit."

Not familiar with this phrase? Let's clarify what it means before we talk about how to achieve it. Product-market fit, defined as "being in a good market with a product that can satisfy that market," was coined by Marc Andreessen, co-founder of Andreessen Horowitz, in a 2007 blog post.[40] While this concept is often applied to startups and early-stage companies, it's relevant for any company bringing new solutions to the market or pursuing new markets—key areas of focus for organic growth.

We find it helpful to have tools to support the product-market-fit process. No reason to invent them! One you may find useful is The 8-Question "Before/After" Grid[41] created by Ryan Deiss. Also, a list by David Skok, a venture capitalist at Matrix Partner, of the key questions to ask along each step of the product-market fit process[42] is handy, along with a calculator template to see how you can score your product-market fit.

Speaking of calculating, it helps to have a way to have a threshold for whether you have achieved product-market fit. We recommend Sean Ellis' approach,[43] in which you attempt to determine the percentage of customers who would either be "very disappointed" if they no longer had access to a particular solution or consider a particular solution a "must have." Your goal is to have at least 40 percent of your customers identify with one of these categories.

If you're focused on fit, you're focused on the customer. In his 1954 book, *The Practice of Management*, Peter Drucker declares, "the purpose of business is to create a customer." In this book, he suggests that Marketing and innovation are the keys to creating a customer, demonstrating he understood customer-centricity long before it was in vogue. Success depends on producing and selling exactly what your existing and prospective customers want. What your customers think they are buying, what they consider valuable, is decisive. This determines what your business is, what you produce, and whether your business will prosper. Product-market fit is the ultimate expression of customer-centric Marketing: your way to truly understand the people you're marketing to and then be able to clearly communicate *why* your solution is compelling to them. The above tips and tools will help you glean a deep understanding of your customers and their wants and needs. In time, this will help you build your products to directly address the wants and needs of your market, allowing your company to grow and evolve with it.

The phrase *product-market fit* includes the word *market*. Therefore, it's important to recognize that your Marketing organization serves as a crucial member of your value creation and innovation process. Creating customer value is Marketing's fundamental mission. Your customers are more empowered than ever and are taking control of how, when, and where they consume products and services. They are less brand-loyal and trusting, and they prefer to acquire information from personal research, friends, and product specialists. These changes have significant implications for businesses and Marketing. For example, you may need to make significant changes in your Marketing mix, messaging, and general approach to customer interaction. In addition, commoditization, the internet, mobility, and virtualization are contributing to a transformation that's affecting companies on a variety of fronts, including new product development.

Customer-Driven Innovation

Without a great product that meets a customer need or solves a customer problem, the rest of the Marketing mix is worthless. While no easy task, the ability to innovate (develop products and services that offer fresh ideas and are relevant to customers) is fundamental to your ability to grow. Investment in incremental improvements to and small innovations for existing products and processes does bring growth. However, it's new, game-changing breakthroughs that will launch your company into new markets, enable rapid growth, provide a platform for long-term growth, and create a high return on investment.

It's vital to get your products right from conception to commercialization. New product development depends on synthesizing the knowledge of what's needed in the market and how to create a product to meet those needs. As mentioned in the previous chapter, Marketing is the keeper of customer intelligence. Thus, it's Marketing's responsibility to help the organization use this intelligence to positively impact new product/service development—by transforming customer insights into innovation-driving business insights. The creation of new products and services to meet the needs of customers provides the basic ingredient for growing shareholder value.

When a company is market- and customer-centric, Marketing plays a key role in the product development process. We believe understanding the problem and the associated wants and needs of the target customers are the first and probably most important steps. Your customers' wants and needs create the relevant link between them and your solution. The more you understand your customers' core values as they relate to your solution, the tighter you can make the connection between how the product will fit into the customer's process and/or life. This is a good place to remind everyone about the important role your salesforce plays in unmasking and communicating customers' needs back to the organization.

The customer's value structure provides critical information for your value proposition. When researching wants and needs, you'll want to understand the "why" as much as the "what." When you can answer, "Why do they want what they say they want?" your focus is on your customers' unfulfilled wants, problems/failures with current solutions, modifications, and benefits. Focus your questions around what customers want. Use the answers to connect the wants to the needs. This process provides insight into the benefit-oriented root wants to help you develop the ideal product that will satisfy unmet needs.

Keen insight into the competitive landscape is also essential to new product success. You must know the category the new product will play in so you can properly identify the competitive set—obvious direct competitors and any product/process that can serve as a substitute for the solution you're creating.

Marketing plays a central role in translating customer information into new products and then establishing these products in the market. New products/services are the way companies respond to changing customer preferences and dynamic competition. Various studies have shown that companies where Marketing and R&D communicate and cooperate realize enhanced new product performance. Over the years, research by authorities such as Ruekert and Walker, Souder, and Song and Parry found that Marketing's participation in the new product development process and its integration with other functional groups such as R&D are among the most important factors affecting new product success.

Marketing Innovation

Coming up with innovation is one thing; bringing it to market is another. Where the neglect of the Marketing mix comes into play is usually in the launch of innovative products. This happens when Marketing is disenfranchised from the product development process. Avoid the mistake of relegating Marketing to the role of sending out a press release and coordinating a new product launch event. Engage your Marketing team from the very start. Expect your Marketing organization to take ownership of the upstream process, which includes segmenting the market, selecting the right target markets, defining the value proposition, and communicating the value to the target markets.

Your Marketing team needs to understand not only who will buy, but why they want to buy and how much they will buy. The team also needs to be able to look with a broader scope and understand when specific markets will buy. These are the Marketing insights that benefit your organization, the kind of insights that can't only make or break your new product, but can make or break your company.

Your Marketing team may need to think outside the box and take a more creative and proactive approach to get your innovative products noticed.

Companies make a myriad of strategic and tactical decisions on how they will operate in the market and engage with customers. There are a variety of factors that affect how well the market accepts your product. These factors could constitute an entire book themselves, but there are three we'd like to address in this chapter: value proposition, competitive differentiation, and product launch. It's important to address these in this order. You may be thinking we should add positioning here. Positioning is a subset of the value proposition and we're going to incorporate positioning into the next chapter.

Your Value Proposition

When marketers talk about your brand or product promise, they're alluding to the value proposition. To understand the concept of a value proposition, we can look at a series of McKinsey staff papers. In 1979, John Forbis and Nitin Mehta wrote in their paper, "Economic Value To The Customer,"[44] that to motivate customers to switch from some other product to yours, you have to offer value beyond the price they're paying—value beyond what they're receiving from the product they currently use. Then in 1981, Harvey Golub and Jane Henry suggested that every product or service gives customers some benefit, for which they're willing to pay up to some maximum price. This is known as the value the customer attaches to the product. Michael J. Lanning and Edward G. Michaels took these two ideas and in 1998 produced a paper, "A business is a value delivery system,"[45] that emphasized the importance of a clear, well-articulated "value proposition" for each targeted market segment. Lanning and Michaels are credited for first using the term value proposition, a simple statement of the benefits the company intends to provide to each segment, along with the approximate price the company will charge each segment for those benefits. A well-defined value proposition articulates a product's actual and sustained performance versus the competition. The value proposition indicates how your product is different and ideally better than your competitors'.

Your Competitive Difference

Knowing the most salient differentiation is one of the most important tasks for Marketing. In fact, Kevin Jones, formerly CEO of Anovia, believes achieving organic growth—the key to success—all comes down to differentiation. He said, "If you're able to create good product, good technology, you've got to be able to find a way to articulate those differentiators between you and your competitors really well."[46] Jack Trout claimed in 2005[47] that the proliferation of product choices in just about every category means companies that cannot differentiate will die.

Differentiation entails clearly distinguishing your product and/or company to make it more attractive and compelling to a particular target market. Companies that do this well create a competitive advantage. The essence of competitive differentiation requires identifying what truly distinguishes your company from competitors. It is the only way to avoid competing on price and the commoditization trap. Want proof? It's in your coffee. Starbucks has taught us all a valuable lesson when a commodity such as coffee became something people were willing to wait in long lines to purchase and pay a premium price.

The only way to avoid the commoditization game is to focus on a source of value as a competitive advantage. Determining this value isn't something you do sitting around the coffee table. It requires a keen understanding of your customers' decision-making process and learning the different reasons a customer chooses one company and/or product over another.

Differentiation plays an important role in gaining customer consideration and preference, two important steps in the customer buying process. So, when was the last time you and your team took the time to consider how your rivals operate or might operate based on the decisions you make? For example, if you brought a new product or service to market, are your competitors likely to:

- Discount their prices?
- Provide incentives to their partners in an effort to tie up the channel?

- Extend offers to customers that will dissuade trial of and switching to your offer?

When customers and prospects can't tell the difference between your company and its closest competitor, it's time for an overhaul. Following these four steps will help you begin to develop your differentiation.

1. **What makes your company and solutions different?** If you don't know what makes you different, neither do your customers. Time for some serious evaluation. Start by evaluating competitors' messaging and positioning. How? Ah, the merits of the World Wide Web. Visit each and every one of your competitors' websites. Comb their sites and start a list of their marketing messages. Read their press release boilerplate and their customer case studies. Note the one or two key cornerstones for each of your competitors. Next, take a look at your messaging platform and positioning statement. If it isn't unique, it's time for a remodel.

2. **How is your difference better?** Different is good only if it matters to your customer. I've always said if companies can differentiate soap, then those of us in other businesses should be able to as well. Here are two examples, one old and one more recent, around how companies in the cleaning industry have found a way to differentiate cleansers. Perhaps some of you remember the Ajax (introduced in 1947 by Colgate-Palmolive) versus Comet (introduced in 1956 by Procter & Gamble) scouring cleaning powders war, where blue crystals that contained bleach helped differentiate what were essentially similar products. Today, we have the Clorox versus Lysol war, with Lysol using the fact that it's safer for food—so you can use it on your kitchen surfaces without having to rinse—as a key differentiator. Discover what customers find important. Differentiation is what separates you from your competitors. This means you need to understand what

prospects and customers value. This is an excellent time to engage your Customer Advisory Board(s). If you don't have a board, engage in customer research to learn how well you and your competition perform against your customers' criteria. Once you have this information, you can define what separates you from the competition.

3. **Keep your promise.** Differentiation is the core of your brand. It's your promise or pledge to the market. Your ability to sustain your differentiation consistently and meet your customers' expectations is what will affect whether customers continue to do business with you or turn to a competitor.

4. **Understand how your differentiation creates your competitive advantage.** Employ it in everything you do. It serves as the basis for how you go-to-market.

Your Product Launch

This leads us to the part of the conversation about go-to-market and product launch. As part of developing a go-to-market plan for innovations and/or demand generation strategies, we consider technology, functionality, customer segments and requirements, channels and partners, pricing, and promotion. Our competitors are doing the same. Therefore, thinking about these questions and areas from the perspective of your competition might provide some insight into their potential opportunities and possible responses. Taking the time to answer the following ten questions from your competitors' perspective may enable you to better anticipate and counteract their moves:

1. What technologies or features might a competitor include to make its product/service more compelling to your target customers?

2. How much of a technological lead must each competitor need in its next-generation product or service to facilitate leapfrogging the current products in the market?

3. How much more will customers be willing to pay for a competitor's technological or experiential improvements?

4. What partnerships could competitors establish that would affect our ability to gain traction and penetration in the market?

5. What customer segments could competitors tap into to accelerate their growth and category share?

6. In what segments will price competition be the fiercest and how big are these segments? What position does the competition have in each of these segments?

7. How can the competition adapt any of its existing products to differentiate them further?

8. Which markets/geographies/customers will competitors focus on to protect their current share? In bringing a new offer to the market? To grow their category position?

9. How will the competition position new products/services and bring these to the market?

10. What barriers to entry can the competition create or develop that could delay our ability to respond?

These ten questions will probably spark more questions for you and your team to address. Reflecting on them will help you sharpen your thinking when it comes to innovation and market entry strategies.

Whether you're using the well-known Stage-Gate process[48] or some other process to guide your new product development efforts, the final stage is always launch. Despite all the efforts in the prior phases, new products have a poor success rate.[49] Only about one in five survive longer than a year, and new product launches are six times more expensive than line extension launches. The result: as many as 95 percent of new products introduced each year fail, resulting in massive losses.[50]

Based on our experience, product failures are often the result of poor product launch planning and execution. Too often, we see a scramble to pull together a plan in the last few weeks or months before launch. Product launch requirements should be part of the signoff process for all new products/upgrades being considered, as both must be funded adequately from the start. This requires input from a cross-functional internal team and perhaps outside stakeholders, such as suppliers and partners. With the launch plan coming together earlier in the cycle, all efforts can focus on ensuring successful implementation in the time period just before launch.

Given the cost to create and launch a new product, combined with the rate of failure, being able to successfully develop and bring new products to market is an important capability. Once you've decided to develop a new product, you'll need to begin thinking about your go-to-market strategy and how you'll launch it.

A product launch won't guarantee the success of a product. A good launch can't overcome a flawed product. However, if you've developed a competitive product that meets a need and is a solution of value, and you can create a believable and ownable position in the market, you're ready to invest in a product launch strategy and plan.

As you begin to develop your product launch strategy, answers to the questions below will help you better develop your approach:

- Why is this product important to your business, customers, and market?

- What role does this product play in your business? For example, does it fill a gap, make you more competitive, or meet a specific customer requirement?
- How is this product better *and* different from competitive offerings? Is the magnitude only incremental or is it significant?
- What constitutes success for this product and in what time frame? Think beyond revenue to such measures as category ownership or position, brand preference, and customer expansion.
- How will you measure the success of your launch? Of course, the primary goal of the launch is to close deals. A well-executed launch should improve velocity; therefore, consider measures such as the rate of product adoption and your inquiry and quote rates as measures of launch success. Take five attributes, such as product complexity, compatibility, relative advantage, observability, and trialability, when establishing product adoption rate targets and timeframes.

Consider Launch Classes

Keep in mind that the launch and product are separate efforts and therefore need their own measures. Also, different products need different types of launches. What kind of launch does your new offer really need?

There are myriad reasons to add a new product to your portfolio. All new products are worthy of being properly launched into the market, but not all products are worthy of the same launch effort. Launches of any kind take resources, people, and cash. It's helpful to have a method to determine what kind of launch is appropriate for what kind of product. The kind of launch should be determined by the reason you're adding the product, its role in your business, and the expected overall P&L impact.

We often recommend you have a method for organizing your new products in launch classes. Different classes merit different efforts. For example, you might create three classes: X, Y, and Z. A Z class might be a product that fills a gap in an existing family of products, offsets some customer risk, and brings your competitiveness back to equilibrium. An X class might reflect products that are innovative and completely new to the market—products that are disruptive and give you a competitive advantage, perhaps signaling a technology change or a new architecture, and/or create a new market. Clearly, there's a difference between a Class X and a Class Z product. While they're both important, your plan level of investment will be different.

Once you establish your launch classes, you can decide how you'll launch each class to your various stakeholders, such as your existing customers and partners; influencers such as the press, analysts, and other industry experts; your internal stakeholders in sales, customer service, and production; your customers who are built-in ambassadors; and so on.

Define what channels and touchpoints you'll deploy for each stakeholder for each class. For example, Class Z launches may only warrant a press release for influencers, but a Class X product may be worthy of a press and analyst tour that includes a briefing kit, beta customer testimonials, and a series of articles. While every class will require a landing page that employs SEO to support the product, Class Z launches may only have a sales sheet and virtual briefing for the sales team and partners, whereas Class X products may need training, a selling kit, and a partner promotion. Once you establish the components for each stakeholder for each class, you'll have a framework for your launch plan.

TAKEAWAYS

- Customer-centric innovation and differentiation are required to grow your footprint, gain market momentum, and accelerate product adoption.
- When a company is market- and customer-centric, Marketing plays a key role in the product development and innovation process.
- Your Marketing team may need to think outside the box and take a more creative and proactive approach to get your innovative products noticed.
- Product-market fit is the ultimate expression of customer-centric Marketing—your means to truly understand the people you're marketing to and then be able to clearly communicate *why* your solution is compelling to them.
- A variety of factors affect how well the market accepts your product, including value proposition, competitive differentiation, and product launch.
- Given the cost to create and launch a new product, combined with the rate of failure, being able to successfully develop and bring new products to market is an important capability.

MARKETING EMPOWERMENT

Encourage your Marketing organization to return to its roots and renew its focus on determining, producing, and selling what your customers want. Use these three steps to empower your Marketing team to lead the innovation charge:

1. Request your Marketing organization own the task of spotting new trends and quickly translating them into opportunities. This requires research.
2. Establish metrics for your Marketing team around innovation, time-to-market, time-to-revenue, time-to-profit, rate of new product success, and product adoption.
3. Enhance the collaboration between your product development and Marketing functions. They need to work together if you want to effectively and efficiently conceive and market new products and services.

EIGHT KEY COMPONENTS TO THE NEW PRODUCT DEVELOPMENT PROCESS (NPD)

Bringing new products to market is a critical aspect for generating value. Shareholders equate value with not how good a company was in the past, but with what you are doing today and tomorrow to continue to sustain and grow value. This means the value of your company is centered on its ability to think long term about the future.

Every company can take advantage of Robert Cooper's Stage-Gate process to develop and evaluate new products. Use the following steps to move your innovation from idea to launch.

Step 1: Ideation

Innovation takes inspiration. Two common analysis techniques employed in the ideation process are STEP and SWOT.

STEP stands for Social, Technological, Economic, and Political—and it's also sometimes called PEST. It's a framework for the analysis of these macro-environmental factors. The social factors often reviewed are the demographics/firmographics and cultural aspects. Technological factors are ones that can impact an organization's ability to create barriers to entry; reduce minimum efficiency production levels; and influence outsourcing decisions including R&S activity, rate of technological change, and automation. The purchasing power of potential customers, the cost of capital, economic growth, exchange rates, inflation rates, and interest rates are often considered when analyzing economic factors. Political factors include government regulations and legal issues. By combining all these factors, an organization can create a view of the big picture. For more about STEP, check out Peter Drucker's book, *Managing in the Next Society*.

A SWOT analysis, which stands for strengths, weaknesses, opportunities, and threats, provides insight into how to match an organization's resources and capabilities within the context of the competitive environment. It is instrumental in strategy formulation and selection. Environmental factors internal to the organization are evaluated as either strengths or weaknesses and those external to it as opportunities or threats. Strengths are represented as resources and capabilities that can be used to develop and/or enhance an organization's competitive advantage (including patents, brands, reputation, cost advantages, access to resources, distribution channels, etc.). The absence of these strengths is viewed as weaknesses.

The external environment analysis may reveal new opportunities to take advantage of unfulfilled customer needs, new technologies, changes in regulations or trade barriers, as well as threats such as new regulations, the emergence of substitute products, and shifts in customer trends. Once the information is gathered, a matrix is constructed. By using the matrix, organizations attempt to develop strategies that will allow them to pursue opportunities that will leverage their strengths and overcome their weaknesses. The matrix helps identify ways to use its strengths to overcome vulnerabilities to external threats and establish a defensive plan to prevent the organization's weaknesses from making it susceptible to external threats. For more on this topic, check out Robert Bradford and Peter Duncan, and Brian Tracey's book, *Simplified Strategic Planning: A Guide for Busy People who want Results Fast!*

Step 2: Screening

Not every idea is a good idea. It's important to establish specific criteria to help quickly determine whether to continue or drop a potential new product or service. Using agreed upon criteria helps eliminate poor projects from the idea-hopper quickly. Even if an idea doesn't turn into a product, keep it in the hopper because it can prove to be a valuable asset for future products and a basis for learning and growth.

Step 3: Concept Testing

As Gaurav Akrani recommends, "Concept testing is done after idea screening."[51] And it's important to note, it's different from market testing. In addition to checking patents and other legal issues, and conducting design due diligence, now is the time to start developing the value proposition, positioning, and messaging framework so you can begin test the concept with existing and prospective customers. The key question to answer at this step is, "Does the potential customer understand, need, or want the product/service?" A product whose value proposition doesn't resonate in the market will not go far. A key part of concept testing is to learn whether potential buyers will pay for the product, and if so, how much.

Step 4: Metrics for Success

The NPD process is an ideal time to establish metrics that will be used to monitor and measure progress as well as success. Include activity metrics, such as average time in each stage, as well as output and outcome metrics that measure the value of launched products, rate of product adoption, and percentage of sales from the new product.

Step 5: Market Test

No product should come to the market before it is primed. Market tests are critical. Testing panels, focus groups, and alpha and beta testing all provide valuable information, allowing for product improvements—not to mention helping to generate a small amount of buzz.

Step 6: Launch Plan

You've perfected the technical aspects of the product. You've honed the value proposition. You have the product processes in play and all the accessories to support the product, such as landing pages, white papers, technical literature, demonstrations, sales materials and presentations, and so on. Now it's time to create the launch plan—which needs to include elements to support the inform/educate, persuade, and motivate stages in the consideration process.

The informative stage seeks to convert an existing need into a want or to stimulate interest in a new product. We'd recommend you build your strategy around informative programs because they're important for promoting complex and technical products. The purpose of these initiatives should be to increase awareness, explain how the product works, suggest uses for the product, and build company image.

Once the product enters the growth stage of its lifecycle, persuasive initiatives will be needed to stimulate consideration. These programs typically focus on encouraging brand switching, changing perception, etc.

Advertising and public relations can be very effective in gaining attention and developing interest and desire. These tend to be less effective at producing action. Sales promotions tend to be more effective at the desire and action stages of the purchasing decision process. Personal selling techniques have the greatest impact on the interest and desire stages.

Step 7: Market Momentum

Your new product is ready for prime time. The product has been validated and you're experiencing market traction. Customers are purchasing your goods or services—perhaps these are early adopters. This is a good time to check back in with the market to understand what's required for the early and late majority and even the laggards to consider your offer. This may require you to make market strategy refinements and build out additional customer journey maps to support your demand generation, customer acquisition, and market share targets.

Step 8: Post-Launch Review and Continuous Improvement

A product launch serves as an opportunity to review your NPD process efficiency and look for ongoing improvements. Most new products are introduced with introductory pricing. Continue to explore ways to continuously differentiate customer needs as your product ages.

New product development hinges on your ability to synthesize customer insights and market intelligence to create an innovative product to meet customers' needs. It's the responsibility of Marketing to help identify product innovation opportunities, gather market requirements, segment the market, select the right target markets, define the value proposition, and communicate the value of new products to the target markets.

Customer & Opportunity Insights
Business Outcomes & Performance Targets
Innovation & Strategy
Segmentation & Positioning
Plan & Execute
Operational Excellence
Performance & Optimization
Org Structure & Culture
People & Skills
Infrastructure, Process & Tools
Data & Analytics

CHAPTER 7

SEGMENTATION & POSITIONING

WHICH CUSTOMERS ARE YOU BEST SUITED TO SERVE?

Organic growth requires a different approach than inorganic growth. To achieve organic growth, you must create competitive advantages, differentiate and innovate your product/service offerings, and zero in on viable existing and new customer opportunities. Once you have market validation and traction, how can you accelerate traction and penetration? This is the focus of this chapter.

McKinsey studied one hundred of the largest U.S. corporations in seventeen sectors[52] and found companies whose revenue increased more slowly than the GDP were five times as likely to succumb in the next cycle, usually through merger/acquisition, than companies that expanded more rapidly. McKinsey found similar results to Cummings in terms of companies growing organically—they outperformed other firms in terms of revenue growth and shareholder value. Upon further examination, McKinsey found no matter which industry the high growth group competed in, the average market growth of their portfolios outperformed those of their peers because these companies tended to focus their growth in the right places at the right times. These firms focused their time and resources on faster-growing segments and introducing new product categories in their industry to achieve growth.

The Need for Segmentation

The lesson here is one we discussed in the previous chapter: expanding organically requires innovation. However, it also requires segmentation—a basic tool for your growth arsenal. Segmentation is the process of dividing a broad target market into subsets of customers, regions, or industries that have, or are perceived to have, common needs, interests, and priorities. In simple terms, the purpose of segmentation is to discover meaningful differences among a target market.

Here's a quick way to test whether you have adequately addressed segmentation. Will the members of the segment react the same or differently to promotion, communication, pricing, and other variables of the marketing mix? If you answer yes, they belong together. If not, you need to revisit your segmentation model. The point is that the segments must be unique and therefore exclusive from one another. With segmentation, your company can determine which customer groups it's best suited to serve and which of your solutions will meet the requirements of its selected segments—and outperform your competition. The purpose of creating a segmentation model is so you can increase your company's ability to grow more effectively and efficiently. Segmentation entails analyzing your current or prospective customers' needs in a more granular fashion to create distinct segments.

Segmentation matters if you want to positively affect penetration and domination. It provides a way to tailor your offer (product, channel, price, and communication) so it's relevant and compelling to the members of the segment. Some of the most common reasons to segment include improving the ability to serve customer needs and sustaining customer relationships across the customer lifecycle. Segmenting appropriately can result in higher profits and opportunities for revenue growth. Through segmentation, you can develop niche strategies and focus your marketing and sales activities on the most attractive opportunities. Executed well, segmentation-oriented marketing approaches can increase your revenue and market share while allowing you to develop strong relationships with your customers.

Most organizations don't have the resources to pursue numerous customer segments simultaneously. So, the most successful companies use data and analytics to evaluate segments, selecting those that offer the best headroom for growth. The philosophy behind segmentation is that members of a segment will respond in the same way to a value proposition and have similar characteristics. You may promote the same product to the segments in a market, but how you position that product to the unique segments may differ.

Your value proposition is the platform for your positioning. You may recall in the previous chapter, we explained that value proposition describes the functional and emotional benefits linked to your offer. In addition, positioning describes why a customer or customers should choose and use your product. How you position the product depends on how you approach segmentation.

Demographic/Firmographic Segmentation

There are a variety of ways to develop segments, all of which should be based on data. One of the most common is using a demographic/firmographic approach. The idea behind this approach is to analyze the demographics for individuals or firmographics for a company of the customer segments where you've gained validation and traction, and then pursue customers that represent those demographics. In the B2B environment, firmographics are used to identify and distinguish target markets based on some or a mix of factors such as size (revenue or employee), geography, industry, etc. Organizing segments by verticals, geographies, and company size are examples of firmographic segmentation. For example, a semiconductor company might organize its business around verticals that provide growth opportunities, such as computing, consumer electronics, and automotive. A translation company might organize around primary languages to support its growth, such as Spanish, English, Hindi, Arabic, and so on. A company in the analytics space might create segments based on analytical maturity, grouping products and services to serve organizations based on their analytics capabilities.

Companies that want to be able to regularly communicate with their customers may decide to invest in a tool that makes it easy to develop and distribute communication to existing and prospective customers. After you complete some research, you determine email is the most preferred method, with video quickly rising as an option. You develop a new way to upload contacts and create emails. You're able to acquire your initial set of customers to validate your idea, and with their help, continue to improve on the offer. Upon examining your customer base, you can see you've gained traction in the hotel industry, especially with luxury boutique hotels. You can take a firmographic approach to this segment and break it out further by the number of rooms, branded versus non-branded, etc.

Needs-Based Segmentation

You can also take a needs-based approach. Needs-based segmentation is based on why customers buy certain products and services over others. In our luxury boutique example, needs-based segmentation might be compatibility with current technology, ease of integration with current systems/networks, and end-customer customization capabilities. Malcolm McDonald and Ian Dunbar have written extensively on the topic of needs-based segmentation.

Needs-based segmentation continues to evolve. One evolution is jobs-to-be-done segmentation. In this approach, you create segments based on the context and use of the product. The idea behind this approach is to segment customers by what job needs to get done and by whom.

You can learn more about this approach in Steven Wunker's book, *Jobs to be Done.*

Persona-Based Segmentation

The "by whom" is a good lead into the final approach we'll cover in this chapter, persona-based segmentation. "Who" can be identified in three possible ways: by role, profile, or persona. It's common that the roles of your buyers are included in the demographic method. A role indicates a job function, the role someone plays within the organization. IT manager is a role. Profiles take roles further. Profiles describe key demographics of a function, such as typical education, years of experience, and job responsibilities. For example, an IT manager would have several years of experience in running regular checks on networks and data security, improving and updating systems, and overseeing and implementing IT projects. You may also require that the IT manager hold an advanced degree in information management, computer science, and/or information technology.

Personas are not the same as roles and profiles. Personas are typically defined as archetypal users who represent the needs of larger groups of customers—think segment—in terms of their goals and personal characteristics. Although personas are fictitious, they're based on knowledge of real customers. They act as "stand-ins" for real customers and help guide decisions about product functionality and design, positioning and messaging, and overall Marketing.

A well-crafted persona enables you to stand in your customer's shoes and take a more customer-centric view. Personas bring customers to life by giving them a name and/or title, personality, and in some instances even a photo. Personas can go across roles and profiles or reflect the nuances of a role. For example, you may have one IT manager persona based on people who prefer mainstream proven platforms, but another for IT managers who are quick to embrace and experiment with new technology—two different personas even though they have the same profile and role. These nuances help you frame your interactions. Different personas, different positioning.

Customers who share demographics may be very different, which is why we prefer needs, personas, and job-based approaches. For example, people in CFO roles may have similar education and responsibilities, but the size or industry may have little impact on how to create segments around CFOs. However, some CFOs serve in a more strategic capacity. Others may have responsibilities for functions outside the traditional finance roles, such as obtaining talent. Still others may be strictly focused on financial planning and reporting. It's often these nuances that impact your ability to engage with a buyer or set of buyers. Every segmentation method requires knowledge about your customers; some methods take more information and the information may be harder to acquire.

Segmentation and Data

As a successful business leader, you're accustomed to trusting your instincts—but it's both an art and a science to create needs-based, jobs-based, or persona-based segments. Regardless of how you decide to segment, you'll need data to help you identify trends and patterns in user and buyer behaviors, expectations, and motivations. Take a data-driven approach for selecting the criteria and evaluating each segment against it. Research is an essential part of being able to segment the market and prioritize your segments. Generally, you'll need two types of research—primary (data you compile, collect, and analyze firsthand) and secondary (data you collect based on work compiled, gathered, organized, and published by others)—to create and select the segments. Conducting solid research takes expertise. If necessary, leverage an experienced third party for your research.

How you segment affects all aspects of your business, including your overall strategy, how you go to market, the partners you choose, your product roadmap, and so on—along with the hard and soft investments associated with these decisions.

While data is fundamental to segmentation, a common pitfall is that many organizations often select their segmentation approach on the data available rather than on the business need. Companies with rich transactional data tend to build behavioral segmentation models (grouping customers based on spending levels, frequency of purchase, etc.). Those companies with a wealth of information about customer preferences develop attitudinal segments.

To avoid this pitfall, you need insights and patterns derived from your external and internal data sources that will help you understand the requirements of customers, how they decide between one offer and another, and what customer and market attributes offer the best fit for your solution. Once you have this data and apply the appropriate analytics, you can form groups of prospects and customers who share the same or very similar value criteria.

When building a segmentation model, clarify the purpose of the segmentation. If you need a way to classify newly acquired customers into a segmentation model, you'll want a preference-driven descriptive segmentation approach. If you're looking to create a segmentation model to support cross-sell and upsell efforts, you'll want a behavior-driven predictive segmentation approach. The former is a more explanatory approach; the latter provides a better way to score and classify. You may need to consider using both.

Prioritizing Segments

Since most companies usually cannot pursue every segment they identify, nor is every segment worth pursuing, you need a way to prioritize the segments and select those that will support your growth goals. We recommend taking a disciplined approach to develop a model you can use to identify, evaluate, and select segments where your company can gain traction and momentum. This means rather than selecting a segment based on subjective criteria, such as affinity for a particular market or salesperson's opinion, you'd build a model using objective data-driven criteria for analyzing and prioritizing segments. This allows you to compare customer and/or market segments on an "apples-to-apples" basis. Here are the four key steps we take our customers through:

1. **Define your filtering dimensions.** The key to building any model is to begin with selecting the filtering dimensions. We like to use two primary dimensions: accessibility and opportunity. Accessibility describes how easy it is to identify market and/or customer segments and how easy the segment is to approach, given the organization's current markets and expertise. Opportunity describes the size and profitability of the target segment.

2. **Establish your criteria.** Once you have the dimensions, you'll need to decide the criteria for each one. To support your growth initiative, consider criteria for the opportunity dimension, such as the number of customers in the segment with a specific set of attributes, the expected growth of the segment, and the expected usage/need for your offer. While there may be growth in a segment, that doesn't mean you can access it. You need a way to determine the ease of access. For the accessibility dimension, you may need criteria such as compliance or standards, the number and types of competitors, how many existing customers you have in the segment, or a technology platform. Establish a weight and rank for each of your criteria.

3. **Gather the data.** After you've built your model, the next important step is capturing the data and applying the appropriate analytics. The data may be something you extract from your internal systems, append from external sources, or acquire from market research. Use it to evaluate and score each customer and/or market segment against the criteria. Then, "plot" the segments along the dimension or use some other prioritizing method to determine which segments offer the best growth potential.

4. **Select your segments.** Those segments that score high on both opportunity and accessibility criteria will be your optimum segments and those you should pursue first. Focus on a workable number of segments.

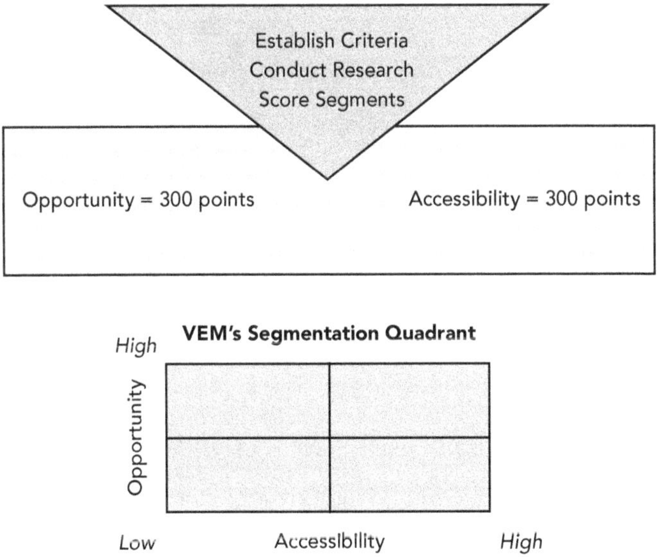

Figure 3: VisionEdge Marketing's Segmentation Model Process

When you complete this process, you'll have something that looks like this:

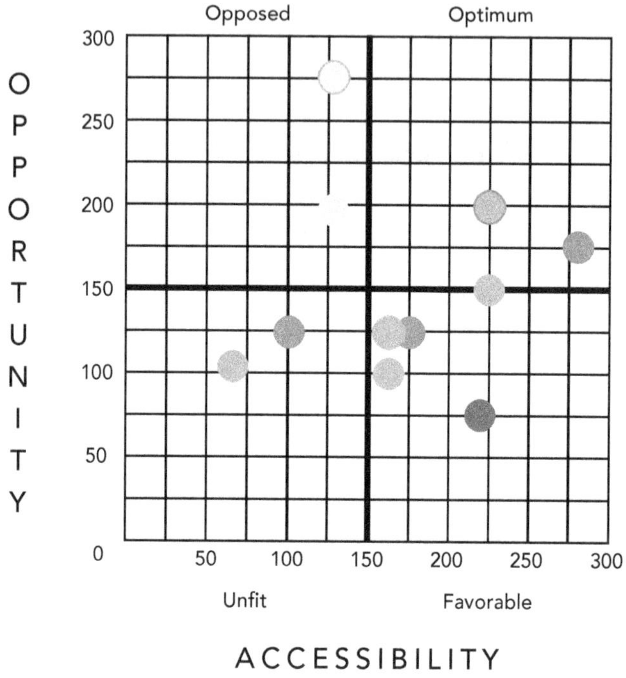

Figure 4: Illustration of Segmentation Analysis. Source: VisionEdge Marketing, Inc.

Here's an option if this approach seems too daunting. Write your list of products or services down one side of a page or flip chart. Then list the types of customers to whom they're sold across the top and put an X in each row and column where each is sold. Most often, this will result in more combinations than you can effectively work with. Match similar items and buying behaviors to create a workable number of market segments to analyze. Focus on the top three to five groups, where the largest overall business opportunities live. Unless there's a significant reason to include a small segment by itself, it should either be omitted or combined with a similar segment for analysis. If you end up combining segments, be sure the new grouping will respond similarly to your value proposition and positioning. By analyzing the products/services and the customers to whom they're being sold and grouping these by similar buying behaviors, you can at least begin to develop a data-driven approach.

Achieving momentum for your organic growth strategy depends on how effective you are at segmentation and the positioning strategy for each key segment. Done well, segmentation both directs and fuels organic growth, ultimately increasing shareholder value and revenue. Achieving these goals requires market and customer segmentation using a data-driven model approach that includes defining the filtering dimensions, establishing your criteria, and accurately and objectively gathering the relevant data.

Don't Go to Market Without Powerful Positioning

You've identified the segments you want to target and the customers you want to acquire. The next step is to be hyper-clear about your positioning. The wrong positioning can be fatal. The concept of positioning is one of the most important components of the marketing mix. Positioning, when properly executed, serves as a powerful aspect of your business strategy. Your company's mission statement and any positioning statement must work together.

Your mission statement generally dictates the organization's direction, vision, and values. It's a formal statement that embodies your organization's culture. As we discussed in Chapter 2, it's the CEO's job to define the organization's values and expected behaviors. Positioning statements bring your company's mission statement to life. When these are inconsistent, you risk creating confusion with customers, prospects, partners, and employees—confusion that will ultimately damage the image and reputation of the company, and lead to lost revenue and market share, not to mention wasted marketing dollars.

Positioning is often encompassed in what is typically referred to as a positioning statement. Solid positioning statements generally include four key components:

1. The meaningful **point of difference** that separates you from others. Positioning requires having a clear understanding of the competitive landscape.

2. A **brand promise** that answers the question: What can I count on from you? This promise specifically responds to what customers want from you—from product features to the feelings they get when using your products. The brand promise must be relevant to the customer and differentiate you from the competition.

3. A **value proposition** that answers the question: Why should I buy from you? It encompasses the promise you're making about the value you'll be delivering.

4. A **concept of singularity** that answers the question: What is the single overall concept I associate with you?

Your positioning statement is the foundation on which all messaging and product positions are developed. When done well, your positioning supports your customer-centric focus. Build your positioning around the attributes your customers and prospects care most about, not those you think are cool and nifty. Be careful about frequently altering your positioning. Once you've found a position that works, you may need to keep tweaking it to keep it current, but think long and hard before completely starting over.

Follow these five proven practices to create successful positioning:

1. **Understand Your Target Market.** Letting the market define your positioning is a mistake. Be proactive. The first step in developing your positioning or repositioning is to identify and thoroughly understand your customer target. To develop a competitive positioning platform that's relevant and differentiated, you'll need to understand core users' needs and wants. If you don't feel you have adequate information about this group, we strongly encourage you to conduct research. (Perhaps revisit Chapter 3 for motivation and tips.)

   Surveying customers and prospects, using an in-depth interview methodology, is the most common way to discover targets' needs and wants, perceptions of suppliers, perceived strengths and weaknesses of these suppliers, and hidden opportunities. Using an independent organization to conduct this research and then listening to the market will give you clear, practical guidance. Understanding your market and marketing to your customers' true needs and requirements will give you an advantage over your competition.

   Internal resources should also be interviewed. Product managers as well as Sales, professional services, and customer support personnel all work directly with customers and prospects and will have valuable insights. Again, an independent organization is best for this task, as their teams are trained to recognize bias and recency-only based input.

2. **Assess Your Competitors' Positioning.** Positioning exists within a competitive context. Therefore, assessing your competitive position is a critical step. It's important because two key elements in developing a positioning statement include a frame of reference and points of parity. Your competitive positioning analysis should explore any companies, services,

and processes that can serve as a substitute for you or your products/services.

You probably have multiple competitors in multiple markets. If resources are limited, focus on the one or two players in your category and market (product, segment, or geography) that pose the greatest threat to you. Conduct a Strengths, Weaknesses, Opportunities, Threats (SWOT) analysis. For each competitor, analyze its positioning statement. See its press release boilerplate for company positioning and key messaging. Make an extensive visit to its website and run Wordle or something similar on its key product and service web pages to see which words are used most frequently.

During the customer research phase, ask prospects and customers who they think are your competitors, these companies' strengths and weaknesses, and how they and their solutions are better and different from each other.

3. **Gain Alignment and Buy-in with a Cross-Functional Internal Working Session.** Once you complete your research, you're ready for the next leg of work—creating your positioning statement. Ideally, you'll engage an outside expert to facilitate an internal working session that begins by bringing key representatives together from across the company. In most companies, there are many differences in how different people and groups perceive and articulate brand and differentiation. Bringing everyone together will provide further insight; help ensure buy-in for the positioning; and support communicating with consistency, internally and externally, going forward.

   As part of this internal working session, you'll want to answer the following questions using your research and your experience in the market and with customers:

- **What is the frame of reference for our brand?** This is actually the most important question and therefore the one you should address first. The frame of reference signals to buyers what they can expect to achieve by using your brand. Sometimes the frame of reference is other brands in the same category and sometimes it's brands in disparate categories. Your product's stage in the lifecycle may affect your approach. New products are often placed within the same category so buyers can quickly determine what the product is. Later-stage products may step outside the category and shift the frame of reference to create growth opportunities. Very established brands may want to shift the frame of reference to preempt the competition.

- **What are the associated points of parity and how can we leverage them?** Once the frame of reference is established, you can think of the points of parity. These are the attributes that give your product credibility and legitimacy. Think of these as the minimum feature/functional requirements your product must meet for purchase consideration. It can be very challenging to fit an innovative breakthrough technology product into a frame of reference and provide points of parity, which is why so many new products fail. The more your product is really a brand extension, the more important the frame of reference. And for established brands, what was once a differentiator can over time become a minimum requirement.

- **What is our point of differentiation?** Points of difference are very powerful. Strong, unique, compelling associations that distinguish your brand from others in the same frame of reference are essential to successful positioning. Example attributes include specific or total number of features, benefits, ease of use, ease of doing business, customer service, and price.

4. **Draft and Validate Your Strategic Positioning Statement.** With the insights from the research and this phase of the internal work, make your first pass at a strategic positioning statement. It should be a clear and concise statement that declares what "space" your company wants to own in the mind of the customers. Your positioning statement should include these elements:

    - Target market for the product/service offering
    - Competitive frame of reference
    - Organization's meaningful point of difference (of utmost importance)

    Take the time to test and validate your positioning statement (Your Customer Advisory Board provides an excellent source of "friendlies" for this purpose. Use the test process to refine your positioning statement.)

5. **Create Your Positioning Document.** Once you settle on a position statement, the next step is to create a positioning document. This document should have a customer-centric perspective and contain at least the following five components:

    1. **Definition**—what you do
    2. **Differentiation**—what makes your company and its solutions different (Avoid basing your positioning on points of difference that can be easily copied.)

3. **Capabilities**—the advantages your company and solutions deliver to your customers and the market

4. **Relevance**—why your differences and capabilities matter to the market and your customers

5. **Proof Points**—evidence that you can deliver on the positioning and the promise

By completing these steps, you'll develop a positioning document that serves as the blueprint for all your messaging and your approach to the market. Use this document to clearly and concisely articulate your value.

TAKEAWAYS

- Achieving momentum for your organic growth strategy depends on how effective you are at segmentation and positioning.
- Done well, segmentation directs and fuels organic growth, ultimately increasing shareholder value and revenue.
- Take a data-driven approach to market and customer segmentation. Consider defining the filtering dimensions, establishing your criteria, and accurately and objectively gathering relevant data in developing your segmentation model.
- Building a segmentation model is something every organization can do. The real challenge is to establish the criteria, gather the data, and apply the process in such a way as to avoid confirmation bias—a tendency to confirm what you already think you know.
- Your mission and positioning statements need to be aligned. Formulate a positioning statement that supports your customer-centric focus. Build your positioning around the attributes your customers and prospects care most about.

EVALUATING YOUR SEGMENTS

Use these ten questions to help evaluate your segments and determine those that provide the best opportunities for growth.

1. How many customers does each segment represent and what is their aggregated buying potential?
2. How do customers in this segment currently solve their problem and prefer to buy the product/solution?
3. How well does this solution solve the problem?
4. Which, if any, of our current or new products/services might solve the problem and successfully compete with the current solution(s)?
5. Which customer segments offer the highest revenue and profit potential?
6. Do we have existing customers in any of these segments?
7. How accessible are these segments?
8. If we could access these segments, how would we position our products or services to reach target segments?
9. How does the segment help us increase our market penetration and potential category ownership? In which of the segments would this be the easiest to achieve?
10. Which segments provide the best marketing opportunity AND return on investment?

Once you have the answers to these questions, you can begin to evaluate the opportunity and accessibility of the segments. This evaluation will enable you select and prioritize the customers who will accelerate your growth efforts.

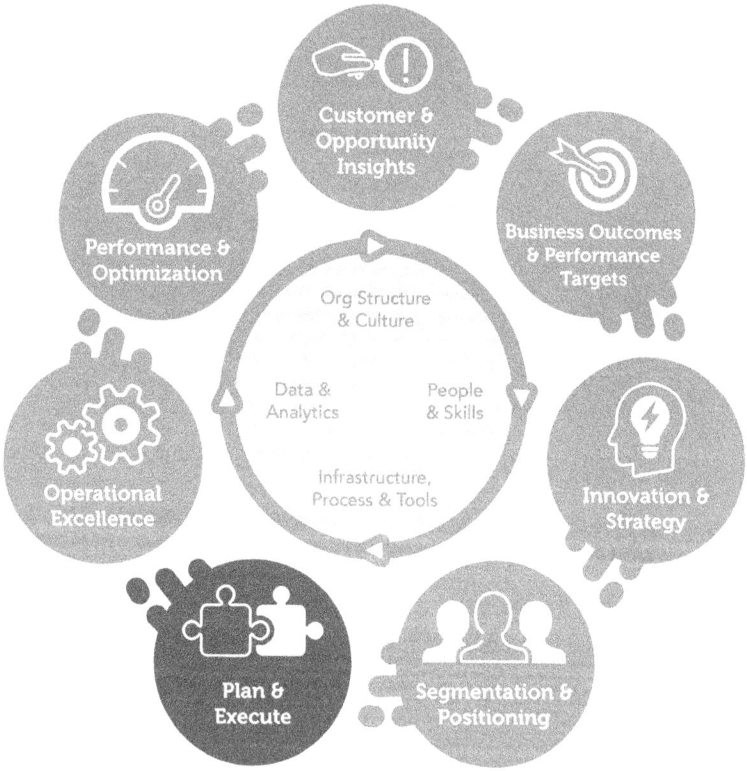

Customer & Opportunity Insights
Business Outcomes & Performance Targets
Innovation & Strategy
Segmentation & Positioning
Plan & Execute
Operational Excellence
Performance & Optimization
Org Structure & Culture
People & Skills
Infrastructure, Process & Tools
Data & Analytics

CHAPTER 8

PLAN & EXECUTE

MAXIMIZE YOUR MARKET OPPORTUNITIES

Rob Adams, former faculty at The University of Texas at Austin's MBA program who's an advisor at CNBC Disruptor 50 Council, has founded or financed more than forty companies—including Texas Venture Labs—that have launched more than one hundred products with transactions exceeding one billion dollars of capital. He's also written a couple books, *A Good Hard Kick in the Ass: Basic Training for Entrepreneurs* and *If You Build It Will They Come? Three Steps to Test and Validate Any Market Opportunity*. I've had the opportunity to hear Adams on several occasions. Every time, I've heard him emphasize how important it is for companies to have market validation for their solutions. He says, "based on the percentage of new products that fail, $260 billion is lost in the U.S. alone. That is dollars right down the drain. What a phenomenal waste of time, effort, capital and business resources."[53]

If you've been completing the work associated with the prior chapters, you know the customer's problem, and you've developed a customer-centric competitive solution and proven its validity in the market, defined your success, selected a strategy, established your value proposition, homed in on a segment, and crafted the positioning for the segment. You have clarity around your destination. Now you need to navigate your course. That takes a plan—your overall business plan, along with a plan for every operation within the organization. Each of these operational plans should be anchored to the same business outcomes—the outcomes you established in Chapter 4 that define success for your business in customer-centric terms.

In this chapter, we're going to focus on your Marketing and Sales plan(s), because these are two of the most important customer-facing, demand-generation operations within your organization. Of course, how well you engage prospective and existing customers—the experience you create for them from the moment they first encounter your organization through the entire lifecycle—has enormous implications on your ability to find, keep, and grow the value of your customers and your company.

The Work of Marketing and Functional Alignment

Marketing is the only function within an organization with the word *market* in its name. Marketing's primary responsibility is to help the company accelerate growth, create value, and improve performance for the sole purpose of acquiring and retaining profitable customers. This is the work of Marketing—all things that serve this purpose. Ideally, Marketing should be informing our organizations which customers and prospects to target, because as marketers, we're the ones who are supposed to identify the best customer and market opportunities from our customer and market segmentation and sizing efforts. Marketing collaborates with other functions in various ways—the customer service/support function, the product/R&D function, the solution delivery function, and of course the Sales function—to help companies, in the words of Peter Drucker, "create customers."

To clarify, Marketing's mission is not awareness and leads; those are byproducts of the work of Marketing. If Marketing has led the organization through the Circle of Traction, it should be able to help the organization and the operations/functions within it successfully contact and connect with existing and prospective buyers; increase consideration for the company's solutions; create more conversations with these potential buyers and the Sales organization; and convert more of the buyers into customers, repeat buyers, and ideally referrers of other customers.

As we discussed in Chapter 4, all the functions and their plans are anchored to the same business outcomes and success metrics—KPIs; every function is aligned to the mission and the purpose needed to achieve these outcomes. The better each function is aligned to the outcomes, especially your Sales and Marketing functions, the more likely each of these functions can positively affect the *demand* variable of the equation. (*Supply* is the other variable.) I recall my early days at Motorola when we were building a microcontroller business. The mission was clear—convert the world from 4-bit to 8-bit microcontrollers and dominate in four markets: transportation, computing, consumer electronics, and communications. Every team, regardless of its function, understood the mission and its purpose and role in achieving it.

Creating Operational/Mission Plans

One of the best vehicles for creating your operational plans is the customer relationship lifecycle. Taking this approach gives you an avenue for alignment by focusing your entire organization around the same set of outcomes: creating, keeping, and increasing the value of customers. Back to my personal example, everyone knew the mission, and as a result, they also knew who the top ten customers were overall and for each market, and what was needed to acquire, keep, and expand the footprint within each of these customers. Mobilizing around the customer relationship lifecycle made it far easier to establish a common set of priorities and customer metrics, along with a common customer-oriented vocabulary.

Here's a quick overview of how you can approach the mission plan, which synchronizes efforts and sequences the related operations to achieve a decisive strategic effect.

- The commander (CEO) determines the layout of the operational environment and provides direction, vision, and guidance to the various levels of his staff and their subordinates to drive planning and execution.
- The commander develops a "vision" for mobilizing his organization and its interrelationships that provides a "design" for the mission.
- The staff (functional leaders) conduct the mission analysis, develop estimates and a strategic concept, and construct supporting plans. It is top-down. No function develops its plan without knowing the overall mission plan.

Using a Customer Journey Map

One essential tool to support creating customer-centric operational plans is the customer journey map. While no journey is entirely visible to you, nor is it linear, your ability to map the journey and then synch it to your internal processes and outputs—not the other way around—is pivotal.

Too many companies try to craft the journey map around how they sell. The key is to craft the journey map around how the customer buys—which often isn't a straight line. The more you can craft a customer journey map around behavior, the better you can use data and employ the scientific method.

Research by firms such as Forrester and Temkin found that customer journey mapping organizations better address opportunities to improve key business results such as product/service adoption and loyalty. For example, journey maps can help you uncover breaking points in your existing processes—those points where prospects or customers ride off into the sunset—enabling you to prioritize process improvements.

If you're not familiar with the idea of a customer journey map, start with the definition offered by Adam Richardson, author of *Innovation X: Why a Company's Toughest Problems are its Greatest Advantage*: "A customer journey map is a very simple idea: a diagram that illustrates the steps your customer(s) goes through in engaging with your company, whether it be a product, an online experience, a retail experience, or a service, or any combination." He highlights that "the more touchpoints you have, the more complicated—but necessary—such a map becomes."[54]

Our approach focuses on what we call the "incremental behavioral commitments" and exit and entry points based on success criteria that indicate a customer is deepening the relationship. These signals are what enable you to define your customers' investigation, identification, evaluation, selection, decision, and purchase phases—and the role your organization must play in each. While it may not be a linear process, every buyer or buying group goes through each of these phases. Some phases (see Figure 5) take longer than others. The key is to understand what your potential customers need in each phase to move forward and what behaviors signal that they're ready to move from one phase to the next.

These behaviors and your role serve as the vehicle for developing your demand-generation plan (notice we didn't say Marketing plan), which correlates to your customer phases. The plan should show how you'll move from initial contact to creating a connection, from connection to conversation, from conversation to consideration, from consideration to consumption, and from consumption to community—where customers become your fans and advocates (see Figure 6). This serves as the foundation for your demand-generation, opportunity management, and customer success processes. Your internal processes are synchronized to your customers' processes, truly creating a customer-centric organization.

This approach will keep your Sales and Marketing teams from developing programs and plans based on what they've done before or on

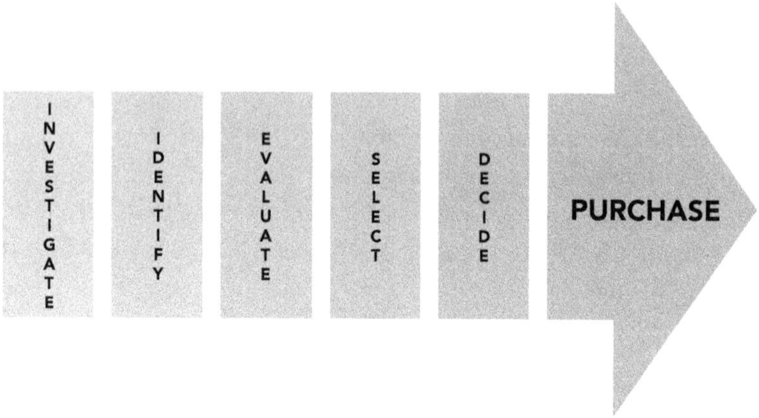

Figure 5: Primary Customer Buying Phases.
Source: VisionEdge Marketing, Inc.

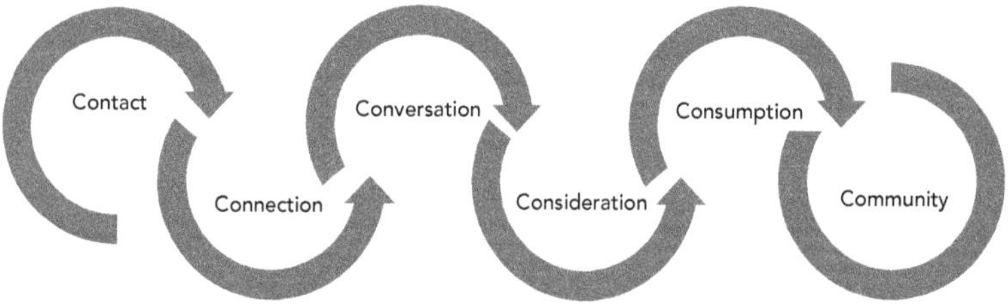

Figure 6: The Six C's of the Customer-Centric Process.
Source: VisionEdge Marketing, Inc.

what they know best, which may be only loosely connected, if at all, to the business. The metrics of success become coupled to the program rather than the broader mission. Consequently, quantifying the value of the program to the business becomes hazy. This outcome-based customer-centric approach to planning flips this problem on its head, creating a top-down perspective. Want to embrace the concept? Start with the business' success factors and the customer journey and work down the ladder. This process reveals what every operation within the organization must each do to support the business, engage buyers, and create a relevant and valuable customer experience through each lifecycle stage.

The Metrics of Success

As a buyer moves from one behavior to the next and from one stage to the next, it's easy to get mired in the conversion measures for each stage. Conversion reflects some type of change. In the world of Marketing, when we motivate someone to click from an email or social media offer to a landing page, or from a landing page to a download, we have achieved conversion. Different conversions have different value, e.g., a newsletter signup does not have the same value as a scheduled appointment. It's important to analyze the conversion data and measures to understand "leakage," when buyers opt-out or leak out. It's important to know the customer buying and lifecycle and the leakage across the journey so you can set customer acquisition and win rate targets, share-of-wallet growth targets, and retention and customer lifetime value targets. (These terms are defined in Chapter 10, where we talk about performance management and optimization.)

Driving growth for the business takes working the numbers, then tracking and reporting on the performance to the numbers. Taking a customer-centric view rather than an internally oriented revenue-centric view and "doing the math" facilitates creating and leveraging a Marketing organization that's relevant; can measure its value; and more importantly, can affect and accelerate organic growth.

Standard Operational Plan Elements

Your operational plans across the company set the course for maximizing your market opportunities. While there's no one way to create a plan, like any roadmap, we believe the following elements need to be standard across all your plans.

1. A section that summarizes market, industry, competitive, customer, and company assessment and provides insight into the actions needed for your organization overall and what the specific function needs to do to capitalize on opportunities and offset challenges.

2. A set of measurable objectives that are aligned with the organization's business outcomes the function is expected to impact. The objectives in some way reflect how the specific function will positively affect customer acquisition, customer retention, and customer value growth. These also serve to articulate the operation's priorities.

3. A clear statement of how the function will achieve each objective. Make sure each statement in some way nurtures the promise of value to the customer. This will keep the customer at the center of every operational plan.

4. Programs and activities with performance targets designed to implement and achieve the objectives. There should be clear and direct line-of-sight between the activities and the objectives and outcomes. Jettison programs and activities that don't support the objectives and therefore the priorities.

5. A calendar and budget that tie to the overall financial model and plan for the company. This section should prioritize the resources needed to execute the plan. Without adequate resources, people, and funding, achieving a plan is as realistic as wishing on a star. Having a stable budget that's completely committed to the strategy enables the organization to operate on a long-term basis, rather than just day-to-day. Growth winners have adequate budgets.

The finished result should be a customer-centric, measurable operational plan that aligns the function with the business outcomes, identifies its objectives, and provides executional guidance that everyone within the organization will understand and support. It's the responsibility of each function's leader(s) to bring the operational plan to life. Think of it as the instrument sections of an orchestra; each plays a role in executing the symphony as a whole. Without the overarching plan and composer's notes, you risk each function playing its individual part—producing beautiful notes that aren't likely to work together. Because each operational plan is anchored to the overall outcomes of the business, it should be clear how the function is connected to creating customer value, growth, and profitability.

Executing the Plan

This is a good segue to the execution aspect of this chapter. A plan is only as effective as its execution; failure is expensive and wastes precious resources. The two common causes of executions that go wrong are lack of communication and shifting focus of the strategy. Forbes Insights has conducted studies on why strategic plans fail and found almost all CEOs say that, "communications is critical to the success of their strategic initiatives and that strategic initiatives often fail due to a lack of understanding, commitment and follow-through by key stakeholders."[55]

Even with communication, there are three other key ingredients for successful execution: alignment, synchronization, and mobilization. These concepts are interrelated, and stellar execution takes all three.

- Alignment refers to the relevant positions of each function with each other and with the idea or goal. Team sports, ballet, theatre, and symphonies all illustrate the necessity of each participant being aligned to the goal and in the right position to perform.
- Synchronization reflects timing. When timing is off, passes are incomplete, dancers fall and trip, and music is out of harmony.
- Mobilization is all about preparedness—a team's state of readiness. This is the value of practice, e.g., training camp before the start of the football season and dress rehearsal before any live performance. Imagine what it might be like if businesses practiced key plays, performed choreographed steps, and rehearsed lines as part of their regular preparation.

Alignment and the Mission

Alignment warrants a bit more of a deep dive, since the lack of it can cause a breakdown between strategy and execution. A study by InsideView, Marketing and Sales, *The State of Sales & Marketing Alignment in 2018: How Leading B2B Companies Drive Growth by Aligning Go-to-Market Teams,*[56] found companies that achieve or exceed revenue goals have 2.3 higher levels of sales and marketing alignment than other companies. Yet Forrester Research, in the B2B Buyers Mandate A New Chart for Marketing and Sales,[57] posited that, "The misalignment between sales and marketing teams continues to be a hot topic, even after a decade of B2B firms trying to solve this problem." As two of your primary customer-facing teams responsible for growth,

Marketing and Sales alignment is crucial for successful execution of your strategy. You may be thinking that of course these functions are aligned. If that were true, the alignment gap would not exist. We decided to see if there were examples of exceptional alignment.

As we looked for examples, we landed on two organizations that provide some valuable insight: emergency response teams and the branches of the Armed Forces. Clearly, when these organizations are misaligned, the results can be far worse than a missed sales forecast. As we examined their structure, a very important concept surfaced. These teams are not aligned to each other. While each branch of the U.S. military must work together, each has a unique mission within the overall mission of U.S. security and peace; each branch serves a very specific purpose and has its own specialties, main areas of focus, and methods of operation. They are well trained and disciplined. They are aligned to the mission. The mission is their joint focus and their joint purpose.

As we delved into the dynamics of these teams, three takeaways emerge that any business can employ to improve alignment:

1. **Forget aligning your teams to each other.** Instead, follow the example of emergency response teams and Armed Forces and align all teams to the mission. Your business has a mission and purpose. Each function within your business, including Marketing and Sales, exists to serve this mission. Remember my story earlier in this chapter about when Motorola was building the microcontroller business. The mission never varied and every team, regardless of function, understood it as well as its purpose and role in achieving it. As a result, we went from a group hemorrhaging and on the verge of being shut down to a billion dollar business that had created two 8-bit industry standard architectures in seven years. There is power in alignment via mission!

2. **Optimize your operations to address the external scenario.** In business, the external scenario is the market and the customer. Taking an outside-in view improves alignment by shifting customer-facing functions from focusing on activity to focusing on which market and customer segments offer the best opportunities and deserve the highest priorities. Staying with the Motorola example, we optimized every strategy and tactic of the organization around the external markets we wanted to dominate: transportation, computing, consumer electronics, and communications. Companies focused on activity tend to take a transactional approach to the business. Here's what that might look like among your Marketing and Sales teams:

> Marketing generates some number of qualified opportunities that Sales then brings to a close. What happens then? "More," not "better," becomes the mode of operating. Sales immerses itself in the latest training and engages in calling on more customers, while Marketing focuses on implementing and coordinating more campaigns and tactics.

However, if you shift your view to the market and customers, the landscape changes. The perspective moves to the point of view of your customers, what they want from you, what they expect from you, and what they can count on from you. An outside-in view forces a move away from a myopic selling perspective to a broader customer relationship lifecycle perspective. The customer relationship lifecycle begins the moment a customer appears on the radar. It continues as the customer moves into the opportunity management funnel and emerges as a customer. Finally, it results in the customer engaging in a variety of experiences that ultimately make the customer an advocate for your company.

The customer relationship lifecycle yields insight into which customers are the greatest lifetime value to your company. Taking a customer relationship lifecycle approach gives you an avenue for alignment by focusing both the Marketing and Sales organizations on the same set of outcomes: creating, keeping, and increasing the value of customers. Back to my microcontroller example; in that company, everyone knew the mission. As a result, everyone also knew who the top ten customers were overall and for each market and what was needed to acquire, keep, and expand the footprint within each of these customers. Mobilizing around the customer relationship lifecycle made it far easier to establish a common set of priorities and customer metrics, a common customer-oriented vocabulary.

3. **Focus on the mission plan.** Emergency response teams create a mission plan from the top down to ensure every effort is tightly linked to the success of the mission. The mission plan synchronizes efforts and sequences the related operations to achieve decisive strategic effect. Here's an example:

> The commander (CEO) determines the layout of the operational environment and provides direction, vision, and guidance to staff members and subordinates to drive planning and execution. The commander develops a "vision" for mobilizing his organization and its interrelationships that provides a "design" for the mission. The staff members (functional leaders) conduct the mission analysis, develop estimates, develop a strategic concept, and construct supporting plans. It is top-down. No function develops its plan without knowing the overall mission plan.

Improving Your Odds

As you can see, execution requires that your organization be able to mobilize people and resources and synchronize itself to ensure the right products get to the right customers at the right time. Synchronization is not easy. It can involve reconfiguring supply chains, increasing knowledge of numerous foreign markets, addressing cost structure, and much more. Communicating the plan to all the people involved and securing their support are critical to success.

Once all the plans are in the place, you'll need to invest in the infrastructure and processes to support them and ensure the entire organization is on board. It all comes down to mobilization and follow-through. Companies that invest in putting the right people in place to get the right things done and emphasize process deliver the best results. Companies that combine attention to process with executive development tend to deliver the best return to shareholders. We like the five steps outlined by experts at Wharton that any company can take to improve the odds of execution success:[58]

1. **Develop a model for execution.** You can adopt Michael Porter's theory of comparative advantage, William Sharpe's capital asset pricing model, or some other model. The important point is to have a model that defines the critical variables to support the successful implementation of the plan.

2. **Choose the right metrics.** Without a doubt, sales and market share are going to continue to be the dominant metrics of business, but there are additional metrics that are critical to monitoring performance and success. Marketing is given money to invest on behalf of the organization. The leadership team wants to know how this money is helping the organization achieve more of something, faster, and less expensively than if that money was directed somewhere else. Use these mandates to guide your metrics selection. For example,

measure speed to penetrating new markets as a way of understanding Marketing's impact on achieving something faster.

3. **Keep the plan center stage.** Once you've earned internal and stakeholder buy-in, initiate a formal process that will keep the team engaged and focused. Meetings between the executive team and unit managers should be regular and ongoing, and they should foster collaboration, dialogue, and problem resolution to maintain momentum. It's one thing to have a strategic plan; it's another to have customer-centric, executable operational plans. Make sure each key function within your organization has a plan and it's aligned to the business outcomes needed to achieve the strategy. Make sure your operational plans are more than a list of activities.

   Organizations without solid operational plans suffer from long sales cycles, weak pipelines, and customer churn. Today, many companies have come to realize that without a plan, they may be engaged in various activities, but not necessarily moving forward. Winners realize not only that an approved plan matters, but the timing of the plan is just as important. A plan approved halfway through the year impedes a winner's ability to make enough impact on the year. In reviewing many plans, one item that distinguishes the winners is the inclusion of a compelling value proposition and positioning platform. (Remember this from Chapter 6 and Chapter 7, respectively?) A well-developed value proposition positioning platform clarifies why people should buy from you and how you're better and different from the competitors they could just as easily select. Develop and live by a value proposition and positioning platform that helps you keep your customers and their problems front and center.

4. **Assess performance frequently.** Annual reviews don't allow the organization to make necessary adjustments. Assess performance frequently to secure real-time feedback on the quality of execution down the line. Studies continue to indicate that less than 15 percent of companies routinely track how well they performed in comparison to their targeted performance. This is a topic in the next chapter.

5. **Communicate.** Wharton management professor Lawrence Hrebiniak emphasizes that effective execution takes excellent communication. It's critical that the people who design the strategy and plan and the people who execute it regularly communicate about its status. You may recall from Chapter 2, where we discussed culture, that growth cultures are data- and performance-oriented because they're typically focused on results. Therefore, these conversation should focus on what's on track and what's not, what's working and what's not, the why behind these results, and any corrective actions to take.

TAKEAWAYS

- One of the best vehicles for creating your operational plans is the customer relationship lifecycle.
- An essential tool to support creating customer-centric operational plans is the customer journey map.
- Driving growth for the business takes working the numbers, then tracking and reporting on the performance to the numbers.
- A plan is only as effective as its execution; failure is expensive and wastes precious resources.
- The best way to ensure strong alignment between an organization's functional areas is to make sure they're aligned around a common mission.

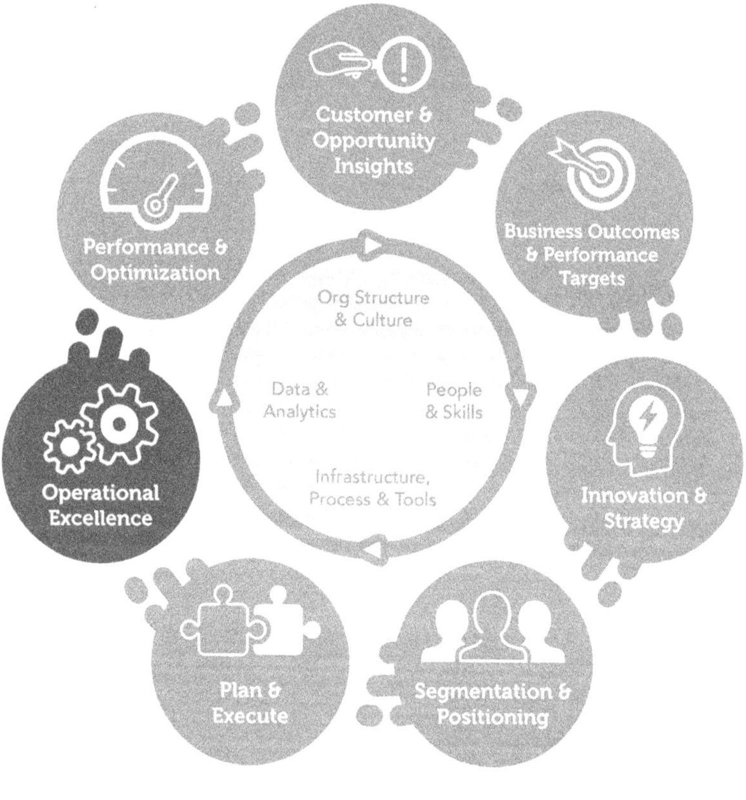
Customer &
Opportunity
Insights
Business Outcomes
& Performance
Targets
Innovation &
Strategy
Segmentation &
Positioning
Plan &
Execute
Operational
Excellence
Performance &
Optimization
Org Structure
& Culture
People
& Skills
Infrastructure,
Process & Tools
Data &
Analytics

CHAPTER 9

OPERATIONAL EXCELLENCE

A CORE CAPABILITY TO SUSTAIN ORGANIC GROWTH

You may recall that Chapter 2 focused on the axle, without which our wheel will not turn. We primarily explored culture, the axle element considered to be the hub. In this chapter, we'll connect the other axle elements to the wheel, as we turn our attention to operational excellence, which is what enables an organization to execute its business strategy. Achieving operational excellence is essential to being able to compete and achieve long-term, sustainable organic growth.

We're not talking about operational excellence as a strategy used by companies such as Dell and Walmart. Their strategy is focused on the production and delivery of products and services to take the category lead in price and convenience, and they aim to reduce overhead costs and eliminate production steps. We're talking more about operational excellence as a way of running your organization. What does that mean? We like the concept offered by Kevin Duggan in his book, *Design for Operational Excellence: A Breakthrough Strategy for Business Growth*: "Operational excellence is when each and every employee can see the flow of value to the customer and fix that flow when it breaks down."

We agree with Duggan that perpetual business growth depends on operational excellence. Operational excellence addresses all parts of the company, especially innovation and growth. We subscribe to the philosophy that operational excellence is a core capability within a company, not a business function. And, in addition to having a growth-oriented organizational culture and access to data and analytics, achieving it depends on the other two elements of the axle, which encompass processes, people, and systems and tools.

Your infrastructure—processes, systems, and tools—is what allows you to have constant rotational speed without an appreciable increase in friction or play. And, what good is a wheel without someone to turn it—ideally, people who are skilled at doing so? Let's delve into each of these elements and how they facilitate operational excellence.

Essential Element #1: Processes

Businesses run on processes, so this is a good place to start. I had the opportunity to be at Motorola when Bill Smith and others fathered Six Sigma.[59] Process is in my blood. One of the key lessons I learned during this time period is that process is at the heart of excellence. In fact, process is one of the four pillars of high-performing organizations.[60] Highly functional organizations leverage distinctive capabilities and processes to improve efficiencies and effectiveness. Firms with highly functional organizations experience more innovation, market share growth, and profit. Planning, reporting, customer journey mapping, segmentation, strategy development, content creation, and opportunity management are all examples of processes—and the list goes on from there. Processes come before tools. Automation is a common goal at many businesses, but if your processes aren't effective *and* efficient, automating them won't improve anything. Adding new Marketing technology if you have broken or inefficient existing processes can become a recipe for disaster. You'll only be faster at following a bad process. It's possible for the purchase of a tool to serve as a catalyst for defining, mapping, and addressing the process if you take the appropriate steps before you use your tool in a "production" environment.

Processes capture the sequence of interdependent and linked procedures used to convert some type of input—typically data for Marketing—into an output. Therefore, *all* work is a process, and you may not need technology to complete it. In fact, we strongly advise defining your process *before* you employ technology. As previously noted, there's no value in automating a bad process, so it's crucial to have quality processes.

Trying to address and improve quality across all your processes all at once may not be feasible, so focus on the processes that affect customer behavior. This is why process is a key part of our work and key to your ability to achieve Marketing excellence.

In 2002, Roland Rust, Christine Moorman, and Peter Dickson published their research, "Getting Return on Quality: Revenue Expansion, Cost Reduction, or Both?," where they categorized processes into two groups: processes designed to drive revenue by acquiring, keeping, and growing the value of customers (externally oriented) and processes designed to improve profit and margin by reducing costs and increasing efficiencies (internally oriented). They found little evidence for the effectiveness of attempting to address and improve both processes simultaneously. In fact, their research revealed that firms primarily emphasizing externally oriented processes perform better than firms that primarily emphasize cost-reduction processes and firms that try to do both at the same time.

Therefore, make processes designed to create customer value your first order of business. Document these processes using process mapping best practices. Process maps visually represent the relationship between the steps and inputs to produce an end-product or service. Good process maps capture all the interrelated activities in the order in which they occur and include who is responsible, when each step occurs, and the dependencies and decision/action points throughout the process. Detail every step of the individual processes. It's hard to identify what to change if you don't have the entire process documented. Beware of assumptions that can get "baked" into your maps. Validate your maps. Only develop new and better steps *after* you finish the initial mapping of the process.

Once the maps are complete, educate every employee associated with that particular process. Make your maps and their associated process flow visual so every person on your team can see how the processes are connected to each other and to the customer. Once your team understands how the process typically works, you can establish standards for each process to reduce variation and improve repeatability.

Essential Element #2: People

We believe people are still the primary secret ingredient in business—that the human interactions between the people inside and outside the company are a critical and discerning aspect of success. Stellar people may be able to muscle their way through without stellar processes. As you build your team, stellar processes serve as the enabler for all your people. Operational excellence drives the relentless pursuit of improved performance across the entire organization. As such, operational excellence requires your people to have a passion to excel and the right mindset. It is people who make your processes and technology productive. Your people need to be smart, committed, and proficient in the skills they need to perform the work. They also need to be proficient at collaboration, communication, and problem-solving. Everyone in your organization should understand the basic concepts of process management, change management, and various quality methodologies.

When it comes to capabilities, experts often recommend building a team with a T-shaped skill set. The top of T is broad skills reflected by all your people and its vertical bar is the deep skills people need to excel at their work. To achieve operational excellence, your people need to have the skills for every relevant circumstance. This is known in some circles as unconscious competence, based on the model created by Noel Burch in the 1970s when he was with Gordon Training International. One of the first books to mention this model was written by Paul Curtiss and Phillip Warren in 1973, *The Dynamics of Life Skills Coaching.*

People work within an organizational structure. Your organizational structure affects how information flows within your organization. The structure establishes the work people will perform and how and with whom they operate inside and outside the organization. The organizational structure for many companies today is created from Max Weber's[61] and Frederick Taylor's[62] management theories developed in the first half of the 20th century. The approach is based on establishing clear lines of authority and control; there is a leader for each occupation/function and multiple layers of subordinates.

In the early '70s, changes in market and business dynamics resulted in a new concept referred to by Peter Drucker as "federal decentralization."[63] Companies were organized into a number of independent units operating simultaneously, each conducting its own activities. As the rate of change accelerated, Peter Senge proposed the concept of the learning organizations, "where organizations are continually enhancing their capacity to create."[64] The structure of companies today reflects a mix of these approaches, attempting to take the best from each. Sometimes the mix works well and other times not so much.

As the Age of the Customer, where "empowered customers are shaping business strategy," continues to dominate, the organizational structure and metrics companies need to survive, let alone thrive, must evolve. What would that look like? Your structure might be designed more around the customer experience. Imagine the implications to your structure if you organized your people into groups that match these key phases of the customer journey:

- Early stage of the prospective new customer as they make contact
- Moves from contact to consideration to purchase
- Purchasing and implementation/deployment experience
- Post-purchase, such as support, billing, and problem resolution
- Loyalty, including repeat purchases, advisor for innovation, and advocate

This approach takes more than changing words on the organizational chart. This is an approach to support the transformation process designed to spur growth and mobilize your organization, especially your customer-facing functions. Modifications to your structure also have implications for how you set your outcomes and establish your metrics. Each customer process will need customer-specific outcomes, with customer equity becoming the overall measure of success.

Customer equity in any year =
[(number of new customers x average revenue of new customers)
– (acquisition costs)]
+ [(number of old customers x average revenue of old customers)
– (servicing costs)]
– (number of customers churned x average revenue of churned customers)

Each experience team would need to establish outcomes that tie to customer equity as the Key Performance Indicator (KPI). Table 1 suggests some possible customer-centric measures and metrics tied to customer equity.

Metrics	Calculation
Net Customer Revenue	Total customer purchases – total customer returns
Customer Lifetime Value (CLV)	Average order total x each customer's average number of purchases per year/churn rate
Customer Profitability	Customer revenue – (known customer-specific costs + a percentage of operating/overhead costs)/customer revenue
Customer Loyalty	A weighted combination of repeat business, influence, and advocacy metrics—or it may be as simple as the Net Promoter Score
Customer Share-of-Wallet	A comparison of a weighted combination of a particular customer's revenue, preference, and loyalty metrics for the company versus its competitors for the same factors
Customer Retention	Number of customers who left/total number of customers
Customer Renewal Rate	Number of repeat customers within a specific time frame/ total number of customers within the same timeframe
Customer Churn Rate	Number of customers lost within a specific timeframe/ total number of customers at the beginning of the same timeframe
Customer Experience Rating for Each Phase	Customer satisfaction score for the specific phase—gathered via post-purchase, post-implementation or customer support surveys
Customer Satisfaction	The American Customer Satisfaction Index (ACSI) database, maintained by the University of Michigan—an excellent starting point for this work
Customer Acquisition Rate	Number of new customers/total number of customers for a time period
Customer Acquisition Cost	Total Sales & Marketing cost/number of new customers added
Customer Conversion Rate Across Each Phase of the Customer Journey Map	Total number of prospects or customers who entered phase N – the number of people who did not move forward to a later phase (i.e., number of people who DID move forward)/total number of prospects or customers who entered phase N

Table 1: Customer Measures and Metrics Tied to Customer Equity, VisionEdge Marketing, Inc. 2018

Essential Element #3: Systems and Tools

Systems and tools are the third leg. Once you have the right people and the right processes, systems and tools help you increase your speed and facilitate your agility. Two CEOs, Kevin Dunworth of Celling Biosciences and Greg Stock of Zenoss,[65] emphasize that speed is a key factor in long-term business success. Zenoss emphasizes the importance of an organization being able "to move at the speed of change; the ability to quickly evolve." Dunworth believes "the guy that does the best is the guy who can make adjustments on the fly."

Speed and adaptability are vital for achieving agility. While agility is more about your operating model and less about your tools, tools help. For this book, we're not exploring the various tools to support continuous improvement. There are plenty of resources out there on this topic. Rather, we're talking about the infrastructure investments you'll need to make for the organization as a whole and then for each function. It may be too late to create an overall plan for all the tools you'll need. If you have that luxury, wonderful. If not, focus on identifying any gaps in tools you need to support your most important externally oriented processes. Check out *The Right Way to Select Technology: Get the Real Story on Finding the Best Fit* by Tony Byrne and Jarrod Gingras.

While selection can be a challenge, so can implementation. The purpose of any technology should be to help you automate a process and make it more efficient. This is why systems and tools come after process. You can't automate a process you don't have. It's entirely possible that preparing for implementation will uncover some of your operational weaknesses. Maybe you don't have an established process for gathering customer insights, innovation, or demand generation. Or perhaps you do have one, but it's ineffective. Avoid giving in to the temptation to automate a bad process for expediency's sake. All that accomplishes is doing the wrong thing better.

Before you implement, make sure you've completed the work associated with the process you plan to automate. This includes your processes for data quality and management, content publishing and distribution, and campaign development and execution, to name but a few. This type of work is not something either the technology provider or your implementation consultants typically perform. Those experts know how the software works and can help you integrate your process into their platform. But they typically don't design or engineer the processes themselves. They expect you to have done this work and that you've accounted for what's needed to engage customers with your process. If you don't have the experience in-house to map out and properly document your processes or gather the customer insights necessary to inform the processes, make sure to establish a budget to bring in a qualified outside consultant as part of the project.

On to Implementation

Once you have your processes mapped and have selected your platform, more than likely you're going to need help with the implementation. The implementation partner you choose is one of the most critical decisions you'll make. Evaluate several different providers before making a selection. In addition to speaking with the references they provide, go to user communities and find references yourself. Ask questions beyond how the provider performed technically; find out a bit more about how it communicates with customers and the processes it follows during implementation.

While conducting your due diligence, consider asking each reference, "If you had to do it all over again, what would you have done differently?" With this type of due diligence, you'll find a good partner—and you'll also have a list of lessons you can apply to your implementation.

Before you dive in, write an implementation plan. At a minimum, this plan should include key milestones, success factors, milestone owners, target dates, and review dates. Be clear in your plan about how the technology is going to positively contribute to the business and how implementation success will be measured. The ways processes, data, configuration, testing, and so on will be addressed during the implementation are examples of milestones. Review the plan regularly. When things get off-kilter (and they will), take immediate corrective action.

In addition, you'll need a plan to support post-implementation to ensure the technology is adopted and deployed. Training, communication, and change management are part of this plan. If you're not accustomed to creating this type of project plan, seek help from either internal or external experts with strong project management and planning capabilities.

After investing in the technology, you'll be tempted to start your implementation right away. Resist the urge—do not start your implementation until you have both plans completed.

To be truly successful and deliver real value to your customers and your business, operational excellence isn't just nice to have. It's the fuel behind creating an agile organization capable of achieving growth and delivering what customers want. All the elements of your axle must work together like a well-oiled machine to keep your wheel turning.

TAKEAWAYS

- Perpetual business growth depends on operational excellence, which addresses all parts of the company—especially innovation and growth.
- Processes, people, and systems and tools are all required to achieve operational excellence.
- Processes are the backbone of every function in business. How well your processes work affects your effectiveness and efficiency.
- People are the primary secret ingredient in business; the human interactions between the people inside and outside the company are a critical and discerning aspect of success.
- As the Age of the Customer, where "empowered customers are shaping business strategy," continues to dominate, the organizational structure and metrics companies need to survive, let alone thrive, must evolve.
- The purpose of any technology should be to help you automate a process and make it more efficient.
- Carefully choose an implementation partner—and be sure to have an implementation plan and post-implementation support plan in place before you begin.

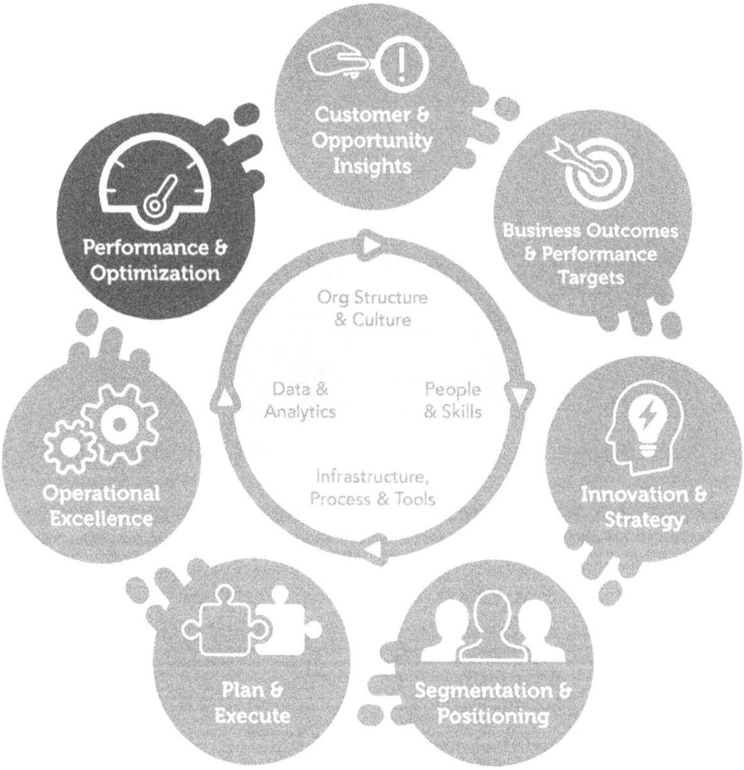

Customer & Opportunity Insights
Business Outcomes & Performance Targets
Innovation & Strategy
Segmentation & Positioning
Plan & Execute
Operational Excellence
Performance & Optimization
Org Structure & Culture
People & Skills
Infrastructure, Process & Tools
Data & Analytics

CHAPTER 10

PERFORMANCE & OPTIMIZATION

WHAT TO MEASURE AND HOW TO IMPROVE ACHIEVING GROWTH OPPORTUNITIES

The focus of performance management is to ensure your goals are accomplished effectively and efficiently. The first nine chapters of this book address the processes associated with tackling organic growth. The essence of performance management is to align the company and its functions around a set of goals. Its definition has remained relatively constant for over twenty years. In their 1998 article and subsequent book, *Managing Performance*, Michael Armstrong and Angela Baron defined performance management as a "strategic and integrated approach to increase the effectiveness of companies by improving the performance of the people who work in them and by developing the capabilities of teams and individual contributors."[66]

A key aspect of performance management is evaluating performance to identify improvement opportunities. In the context of this book, that means improving your ability to identify, pursue, and achieve growth opportunities. In the domain of organizational development, performance is thought of as actual results versus desired results. Therefore, to optimize performance, you need to know what to measure and how well your organization is performing against the measures. The topic of selecting the right measures and performance management has been the focus of two of our previous books: *Measure What Matters: Reconnecting Marketing to Business Goals* (no longer in print) and *Metrics in Action: Creating a Performance-Driven Marketing Organization*. Still, there is plenty to say about this topic.

Companies use several overall financial metrics to measure growth. As part of the growth engine, your customer creation and growth functions (Sales, Marketing, Service, etc.) have the opportunity to impact real revenue growth (revenue after overall increases or decreases in the profit index) and sustainable revenue growth (how much additional revenue growth your company can handle). The leaders in these functions need to think beyond typical measures and metrics, such as leads generated, meetings held, and service tickets resolved, to more outcome-oriented metrics around their contribution to the rate, cost, and number of acquired customers; the rate of growth of specific customers; and share-of-wallet, advocacy, and referral growth among customers.

One characteristic that distinguishes customer-centric organizations is they understand revenue comes from customers. They recognize they don't market to or service buckets of revenue. Focusing on revenue is an internal point of view. One of the ways we can tell whether a company is customer-centric is how well it can relate the number of customer "deals," whether from new or existing customers buying which products/services comprising the revenue number. Two important measures associated with the "deal" part of the equation are the rate of profitable customer acquisition, especially net new customers (those you're doing business with for the very first time) and win rate. The customer acquisition rate is relatively simple—it represents how fast you acquire customers, ideally profitable ones. It's hard to stay in business for long, let alone grow, if your cost to acquire is more than the customer is worth in the short or long term.

A related measure of acquisition is win rate. It's actually a ratio that provides a view into the number of customers in the consideration stage who purchase. Win rate is an indicator of Marketing and Sales alignment and effectiveness as well as your ability to successfully compete. It will be hard to grow if customers are heading out the back door. This is why once you acquire customers, achieve market validation, and are on your way to category ownership of the space in which you compete, you need to monitor three broad customer metrics that have financial implications tied to growth: share-of-wallet, customer stickiness, and customer lifetime value.

Share-of-Wallet

Growth comes from acquiring new customers as well as expanding your footprint with an existing customer. This expansion can be a result of a customer buying more of a product it already purchases to address an increase in volume, buying more of product it already uses to embrace a completely new application, buying additional products it's not currently purchasing from you, or some combination of these situations. The notion of an existing customer buying more falls into what's referred to as the share-of-wallet.

The total amount a customer can spend in a specific product category is known as the customer "wallet." The share-of-wallet, then, is how much a customer spends with a particular seller. The simplest way to calculate the share-of-wallet is to measure how much of a customer's total category spending you own versus what the customer spends in that category and then compute the resulting ratio.

Using share-of-wallet as a metric improves your understanding of where added value may exist among your existing portfolio of customers. By understanding the total wallet and the share-of-wallet, you can identify which customers are the most loyal and which have the greatest growth potential. Both the ratio and the actual difference are important; the first tells us the share-of-wallet, the second the potential value.

Customer Stickiness

Most research[67] supports the claim that acquiring new customers is more expensive than retaining current customers. Some studies suggest that a 2 percent increase in customer retention has the same effect on profits as cutting costs by 10 percent, and a 5 percent reduction in customer defection rate can increase profits 25 to 125 percent, depending on the industry. There is solid data that suggests companies with high retention also grow faster. Therefore, you need to know how "sticky" your customers are.

You can determine your stickiness by measuring and monitoring your customer churn and retention rates. A simple way to calculate churn is by calculating the number of customers who discontinue a service during a specified time period divided by the average total number of customers over that same period.

Churn Rate = Customer loss during a specific period
÷ total customers at the start of the period

While it's important to understand the rate at which you're losing customers, you'll also want to calculate the revenue lost, or churned, as a result.

The customer retention rate calculation is slightly different. Take the number of customers at the end of specific point in time and subtract any new customers acquired in this same time period. Divide this number by the total number of customers at the start of the time period and multiply by one hundred.

Retention Rate =
[(Number of customers at the end of a time period)
– (Number of customers acquired during the time period)
÷ (total number of customers at the start of the time period)]
x 100

The key is knowing how many are defecting and why, as well as how many are staying and why. The reasons customers leave and why they stay are often different, and customers don't necessarily leave for the exact opposite of the reason they stay. For example, customers might stay because switching is extremely difficult. Or, they might choose to leave because the technical support is poor. It's important to work both sides of the equations.

Customer Lifetime Value

Without customers, there is no business. Therefore, customers are a company's most valuable asset. The longer a customer is a customer, the more valuable that customer is and the more value that customer creates in terms of real revenue and (you hope) referrals. Customer Lifetime Value (CLV) is a measure that reflects the value of the customer over the customer's lifecycle. CLV represents the value of your organization's relationship with the customer. Determining which types/profiles of customers produce the highest CLV helps you determine in which existing customers to invest.

There are various approaches for calculating CLV. At its core, CLV is built from the following equation:

CLV = (Frequency of Purchase)
x (Duration of Loyalty) x (Gross Profit)

Compared to their competitors, best-in-class organizations are significantly better at impacting this metric.

These are just a few of the critical measures. There are certainly other customer-centric and growth measures, for example, market value index (which helps you understand how your company compares to other companies on attributes important to the customer), customer vulnerability index (a valuable metric for understanding which customers are succumbing to competitive pressure), and service quality measures. You don't need all these measures. Select the measures most tightly linked to your outcomes.

Circling Back to KPIs

The measures and metrics in this chapter can become the basis for your organization's Key Performance Indicators (KPIs), something we discussed in earlier chapters. The simplest way to think of KPIs is to consider these the metrics that your organization is willing to spend money on to improve. The KPIs become the basis for how you measure the success of the organization and they are the foundation for the metrics and measures for each function and person in the organization charged with driving growth.

Being able to measure success is going to take identifying and collecting data and analyzing this data. While the skills for data and analysis discussed in Chapter 3 are the same, how they are applied here is different. The focus in this instance is on establishing ideal performance parameters, evaluating actual performance against the parameters, and then determining what action is needed as a result.

To accomplish this, you'll need to understand how to connect everyday work to the KPIs. The ability to create this connection typically requires forming a chain between the KPIs and the function's objectives, programs, and activities. We call these value-impact metrics chains. Once you can establish the metrics and craft the chains, you're well on your way to developing scorecards and dashboards. Both tools are intended to help you measure and optimize performance.

The Value of Debriefing to Optimize Performance

Marc Hafner is an award-winning CEO who he has more than twenty-five years of experience successfully driving and leading growth for organizations ranging from startups to large Fortune 500 divisions. Since 2010, he's been at the helm of Revionics, an Austin-based company founded in 2002 that provides the retail market with predictive analytics. Hafner believes organic growth "is where you establish the foundation for the company's future growth plans. It's extremely critical that you get that right, first and foremost before attempting any grand inorganic growth plans."[68] He says that like all successful sports organizations, "business organizations are successful because they're willing to accept that they're not perfect, they go back and review what happened, make changes as necessary, and move on." The Revionics team embraces the idea of the "game review," where "we review the game film on things that are good and we review things that are bad." A game review provides an opportunity to pause and address how to make things better, that is, optimize performance.

The key message here is to make and take the time to debrief. Continuous improvement and performance management are crucial to achieving a winning season. We know that with such busy schedules, it's easy to forgo this step. We urge you not to skip the game review. Because we're all busy, schedule your debrief meetings in advance. We recommend setting aside ninety minutes for these meetings within one to two days after the results are calculated, incorporating these five steps into your game review to focus on improvement:

1. Start with a recap of the growth strategy, objectives, program in play, and performance target.

2. Present the results.

3. Move into the "dissection" phase of the meeting. Review all the "plays" and what worked and what didn't and why.

4. Document lessons learned, what to repeat, and what to do better/differently. Consider where to incorporate these in the Circle of Traction. Is there a need for some additional customer insights or competitive intelligence? Does there need to be change to the way outcomes are created and stated? What is the impact on strategy formulation, innovation, and/or segment selection?

5. Revisit your upcoming programs associated with the objective and strategy and adjust them based on your session output.

Performance Management Practices

Frederick Winslow Taylor is credited with starting the Scientific Management movement. He and his associates studied how work was performed. They examined how the performance of work affected worker productivity. In his book, *The Principles of Scientific Management*, published in 1911, Taylor discussed his philosophy based on the belief that making people work as hard as they could was not as efficient as optimizing the way the work was done. While a lot has happened in the past one-hundred+ years, many of the performance management systems have remained fundamentally the same, despite the increased complexity of work and the volume of performance data.

Performance management practices are shifting from backward-looking, activity-based evaluations (how much work is delivered on time) to fact-based performance evaluations that link the work of people to their impact on the business. While this is a worthwhile shift, it only works if people understands how their work ties directly to a business outcome. However, some experts in the organizational development field suggest that KPIs now actually account for less than 5 percent of how employee performance is evaluated. Clearly the success of your people and your company in achieving organic growth is to have clear performance targets.

All the measures in the world, and there are certainly an abundance of them, are for naught if we don't use them to optimize and improve performance. I can't think of any leadership team that doesn't have a cadence for each function to report on performance. (If you know of one, please send them our way.) To put performance back into management, you need to know how the different areas of your business and your people are performing. To excel at performance management, organizations need to develop and implement methods and tools that ensure the feedback, accountability, and documentation necessary for them to achieve the desired outcomes.

Using Scorecards and Dashboards

Scorecards and dashboards are two vital tools that support performance reporting. People often use these terms interchangeably, but they are different. Scorecards keep score. If you've ever played regular or miniature golf, you're probably familiar with the golf scorecard. Each player is issued a card on which the performance target for each hole is identified. The goal of the player is to achieve or beat the performance target. A player's strokes for each hole are tallied to a total score for the round, and each player competes against the course and the other players.

In the business world, when you track qualified leads against the performance target set for a Marketing program or programs, you're keeping score. A scorecard reports on qualified leads generated by each program for a set time period. As golfers score their play over multiple rounds, they earn a handicap, which is a numerical measure of a golfer's potential ability. Conversion rate and win rate reflect similar measures for Marketing.

A popular business scorecard is the balanced scorecard, created to help organizations translate strategy into measures that communicate a company's vision A study by Cranfield University[69] showed that more than 50 percent of large enterprises use some type of a balanced scorecard, which provide a framework for integrating measures derived from strategy. The idea behind the balanced scorecard introduced by Robert Kaplan[70] is that strategies can be aligned with key performance objectives to optimize performance and opportunities. Balanced scorecards serve as an important tool on a number of fronts. Organizations use them to:

- Clarify and gain consensus about strategy
- Communicate the strategy throughout the organization
- Align business unit goals to the strategy
- Link objectives to long-term targets and annual budgets
- Identify and align strategic initiatives
- Provide a strategy review process

With a balanced scorecard, the corporation, down to each organizational unit and even to the individual level, can:

- Understand the key performance indicators they have control and responsibility for and the relationship to the overall success of their organization

- Have visibility into operations and issues of all business units and enable the management team to easily monitor and understand how the organization is progressing against plan

- Enable the implementation of and ability to track key initiatives for addressing problem areas or pursuing business opportunities

- Use a strategic feedback and enterprise communication platform

Scorecards keep a tally of your score against a desired performance target, providing a snapshot of performance, but they won't tell you why your efforts resulted in the final score. This is the purpose of a dashboard. If you want to understand the *why* behind your outcomes and facilitate decisions, you need a dashboard. We can use the games of golf or bowling to continue to clarify the difference. The scorecards used in these games help you chart your progress for that specific game against the ideal score; in golf, par is 72 and in bowling, the highest possible score is 300. You can see how you're performing. But the score alone won't help you know what to change to improve performance. This is the realm of a dashboard. Dashboards provide an operational view and comprise multiple measures that are related to each other. Continuing with the golf example, we can craft a dashboard of the information a golfer might employ, such as driving distance, fairways hit off the tee, and putts per hole, to gain insight into his performance compared to the competition.

Using measures that are in the context of industry standards or performance targets, a dashboard helps organizations understand where they are performing well and what improvements need to be made to achieve the desired outcomes. Determining which measures are on your dashboard depends on how the success of these outcomes will be measured. For example, to understand how to increase market share or grow category ownership, you need a dashboard that provides insight into win rates, new product adoption, and referral rates.

The test of a good dashboard is how well it helps you answer questions like these:

- Can we tell what is and isn't working?
- Are we moving the needles expected of us and if so how far?
- Are course changes needed and if so what are the best options?
- What is our level of risk?

The trick in building and leveraging this type of dashboard for decision-making, risk management, and course adjustment is to be able to separate the signals from the noise. When the signal-to-noise ratio is poor, your signal (in this case your salient information) gets lost in the noise (all the background data). Too much data is one of the primary culprits of noise. This is why it's important to remember that any dashboard needs to answer the proverbial question: So what? If it doesn't facilitate an action or a decision, what is its purpose? Think about the dashboard of your car—there is a lot of data, but it all serves a specific purpose. The speedometer lets you know what your speed is so you can decide whether to stay within the speed limit. Your fuel gauge lets you know how much fuel you have so you can decide if you need to refuel now or later. Your average-miles-per-gallon data gives you information so you can decide whether you're receiving enough value for your money. You won't necessarily produce a higher-quality dashboard by simply reducing the amount of data (lowering the noise level). You need to have the right data to help make decisions and actions that will improve and optimize performance. Select *only* the data for your dashboard that is relevant to these.

The Need to Change

Your scorecards and dashboards can indicate that change is warranted to optimize and improve performance. Often, this is where the wheel stops turning—when it meets resistance to change. The size or industry of a company doesn't matter.

Organizations often underestimate the effort required to grow—they want something fast and easy. It reminds me a little of people who want to lose weight, but they don't want to make any activity or diet changes. They want to take a pill, preferably while they sleep, and watch the pounds quickly melt off.

Unfortunately, such a magic pill doesn't exist. Even the diet pill companies clearly state, "X pill was designed to be used in conjunction with a healthy diet and exercise. Some users may lose weight without changing their diets or exercising, but exercise and healthy eating are recommended for optimal results." And there you have it, most of us who want to lose weight are going to have change—change our diet and/or change our exercise routine.

Change is pervasive in our society and a fact of life in organizations. Change involves making alterations to the organization's purpose, culture, structure, and processes in response to seen or anticipated changes in the environment. This means you must keep the axle in good working order. Change facilitates prosperity and growth, even in volatile, uncertain, complex, and ambiguous environments.

Here are five vital steps to affect change:

1. **Link change explicitly and tightly to real performance outcomes.** Change is not intended for the sake of change; it should improve business performance. The result of change should generate specific and quantifiable business outcomes.

2. **Create concrete initiatives.** These initiatives should support the outcomes and focus on what it will take for them to affect the organization's operation in a positive way.

3. **Include human dimension in your calculations.** People do what people do. They embrace, resist, obstruct, and rise to the occasion. So listen, a lot. People dodge drafts. Find ways to enroll people into the process.

4. **Develop and market the message.** When we sell to different market groups, we develop appropriate campaigns. Employ this approach internally. Segment your internal markets and tailor the message accordingly. Leverage informal and formal networks.

5. **Recognize that disruption is an important part of the process.** Those who lead change are often referred to as change agents—and being a change agent means you're going to cause discomfort to the people around you. You're going to interrupt the "way we do things." As a change agent, you must be able to step outside your own comfort zone if you want to take people outside of theirs. The key to being a change agent is producing and keeping a healthy tension alive in the organization.

Effective strategic business leaders realize change is part of the continuous improvement process—the drive to optimize performance. CEOs bent on survival and dedicated to growth embrace change and help their organizations adapt.

TAKEAWAYS

- To optimize performance, you need to know what to measure and how well your organization is performing against the measures.
- Three broad customer metrics have financial implications tied to growth: share-of-wallet, customer stickiness, and customer lifetime value.
- The measures and metrics in this chapter can become the basis for your organization's KPIs, with a focus on establishing ideal performance parameters, evaluating actual performance against the parameters, and then determining what action is needed as a result.
- Scorecards and dashboards are two critical tools for optimizing and improving performance.
- Change is a difficult but necessary step in the process of working toward prosperity and growth.

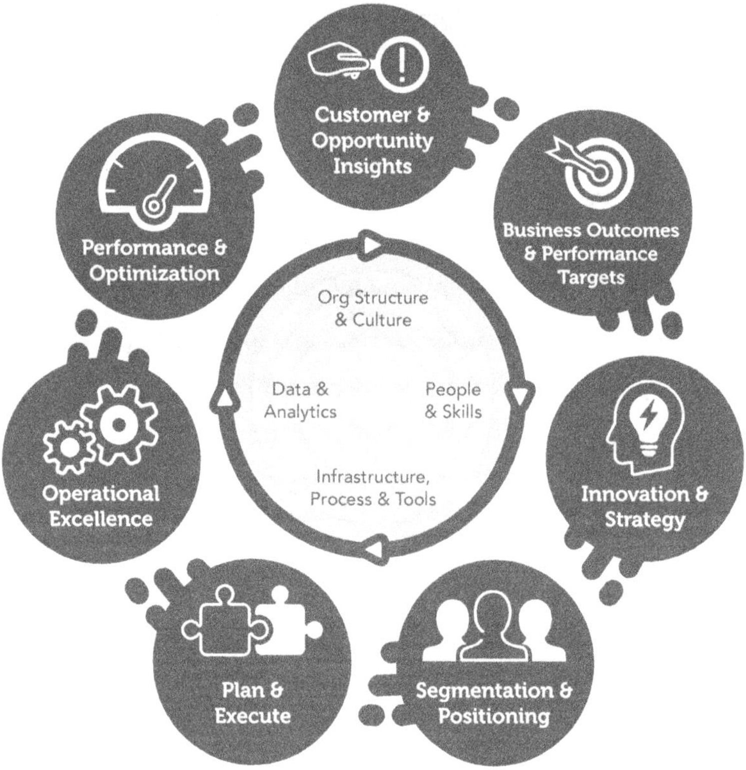
Customer &
Opportunity
Insights
Business Outcomes
& Performance
Targets
Innovation &
Strategy
Segmentation &
Positioning
Plan &
Execute
Operational
Excellence
Performance &
Optimization
Org Structure
& Culture
People
& Skills
Infrastructure,
Process & Tools
Data &
Analytics

CHAPTER 11

COMING FULL CIRCLE

CHOOSE CUSTOMER-CENTRICITY TO FUEL ORGANIC GROWTH

As we come to the end of *Fast-Track Your Business*, we hope we've provided you with some valuable insights and suggestions to help you accelerate your organic growth and realize taking a more customer-centric approach is a critical part of the equation. We know customer-centricity is among one of the most popular topics among today's business leaders, as companies explore ways to increase market momentum, customer share, and new product adoption. Given this focus, it's surprising that the majority of the Fortune 500 firms organize their top divisions around internal criteria,[71] i.e., product groups, functional areas. Operational functions are streamlined internally, but cover multiple customer groups externally.

The Wheel Revisited

We wrote this book for organizations passionate about achieving and maintaining organic growth. We believe it should be your organization's mandate and mantra. We also believe being customer-focused is the secret ingredient in what fuels the growth engine. And while every part of your organization needs to reflect this focus, companies that emphasize upstream Marketing improve their odds of success

(Chapter 1). To grow, you need a deliberate approach that enables you to move forward faster and with more force. It's in this context that we created the Circle of Traction model on which this book is based.

Wheels need axles to turn and the Circle of Traction is no exception. We devoted Chapter 2 to presenting the components of the axle—Organizational Culture & Structure; People & Skills; Infrastructure, Process & Tools; and Data & Analytics—with particular emphasis on the important role culture plays. Only with that foundation in place will your organization be successful as it navigates the external elements of wheel.

If you believe—like we do—that the purpose of any business is to create a customer, insights into customers and the market must be the first spoke in your wheel. Thus, Customer & Opportunity Insights is the focus of Chapter 3. Armed with those insights, you can define what your organization needs to achieve to declare success, the subject of Chapter 4, Business Outcomes & Performance Targets.

After these foundational chapters, we got on roll in Chapters 5 and 6 as we turned our attention to the weighty areas of Innovation & Strategy. With clarity around strategy, you can now select specific markets and customers to pursue, covered in Chapter 7, Segmentation & Positioning. Chapter 8, Plan & Execute, is where we moved into high gear with a focus on the critical areas of planning and execution.

To complete our wheel, Chapter 9 covered Operational Excellence, which is what enables your ability to be effective and efficient, and Chapter 10 delved into Performance Management and Optimization, which is what helps you keep the wheel in perpetual motion.

Each of the elements of the wheel is important in its own right, and you can't skip forward or skip any steps if you want to truly have the best chance to achieve the organic growth you seek. Once your organization understands the value of the Circle of Traction and sees the results that can be achieved by following it, it may become one of its most important tools.

Before We Go—Final Thoughts on Customer-Centricity

Throughout this book, we've tried to connect everything a company needs to do to drive growth forward, with particular emphasis on being more customer-centric. Now that we've come full circle, we leave you with a few final and important thoughts about customer-centricity.

First, customer-centricity is essentially reversing the value chain. (See Figure 7.) We've tried to emphasize the difference between being customer-centric and product-centric. One way to understand the different is to revisit Don Peppers' explanation:[72]

- Product-centricity starts with having a product or service that responds to customer needs and then getting as many customers as possible who have these needs.
- Customer-centricity starts with the individual customer and aims to meet the needs of that customer everywhere (all divisions) and as much as possible.

Reversing the value chain has enormous implications to your business activities and processes. The traditional value chain is product-centric. The market- or customer-centric strategy holds the informed knowledge of the customer and the marketplace at its heart. Shifting to a customer-centric position calls for moving from designing, making, and selling the product or service to choosing, delivering, and communicating the product's or service's value.

As noted while journeying around the Circle of Traction, reversing the value chain means you start with the customers' needs and priorities—and that requires data. Some of this data may be at your fingertips, but you also may be required to conduct research that involves, for example, surveying prospective customers, conducting focus groups, and creating Customer Advisory Boards.

Reversing the value chain will also set you on the path to identify the channels that best deliver what customers need. This may mean you'll need to revisit how you go to market and with whom. And finally, reversing the value chain means you'll need to determine the products or services best suited for these channels, and then develop the resources required to deliver the offerings that will ensure value to the customer.

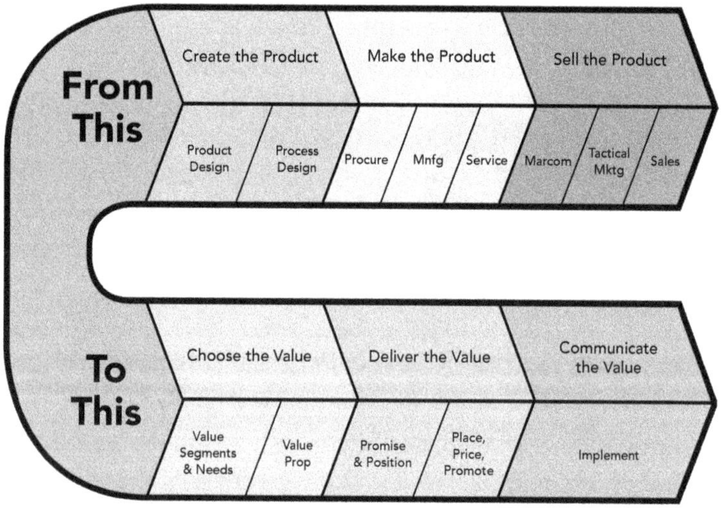

Figure 7: Reversing the Value Chain
Contrast the different approaches between the traditional and reversed value chain.
Source: VisionEdge Marketing

Second, there's no doubt that being customer-centric makes sound business sense. Research has found that companies adopting a customer-centric culture, metrics, and processes improve relational and financial outcomes.[73] A Deloitte study[74] showed customer-centric companies were 60 percent more profitable compared to companies that were not focused on the customer. And a Booz Allen study[75] found businesses that are successful at customer-centricity outperform industry peers two-to-one in revenue growth and generated margins 5 to 10 percent above their competitors.

Third, if you're a product-centric company attempting to transform into a customer-centric one, be aware that this transformation comes with a cost. However, if you want your organization to be aligned around customer commitment and relationships, and enhance your customer knowledge, a customer-centric approach is warranted.

Fourth, identifying what the customer values takes place well before the selling stage. This approach demands that you determine the best strategies to provide value to the customer.

Lastly, the transformation to a customer-centric company means more than changing how you market to your customers. It means you change how you operate your company. It will most likely mean a change in your culture and will certainly necessitate extensive internal collaboration. We touched on some of these changes throughout the book, but they're important enough to warrant more scrutiny.

1. **Customer orientation**. To begin, you and your team will need to move from a transactional orientation toward customers to a relationship orientation that encompasses the entire customer lifecycle. This has implications from how you're organized and how you develop solutions to how you market, sell, and serve your customers. The focus is no longer on creating discrete customer transactions, but on creating ongoing holistic customer experiences across the customer lifecycle.

2. **Solutions versus selling**. A customer-centric transformation means you leave the world of selling "products" for the world of solving problems. How well you understand and can profitably solve customer problems serves as the basis for your decisions: what you develop, how you go to market, and the partners you choose.

3. **Front-line versus top-down driven**. Your customer interaction and experiences occur on the front line. The interaction and therefore the action is with your Sales, Marketing, and Service personnel. You'll need to make sure these people have the skills, resources, and authority to manage "moments of truth."

4. **Engineer or reengineer business processes**. This step is probably one of the most difficult and expensive aspects of the transformation. If you want your transformation to be more than window-dressing, you'll need to "bite the bullet" and very likely rework every business process.

Companies that successfully reverse the value chain and make the transformation reap a number of rewards, starting with creating more value for their customers, brand, and product. The internet has leveled the distribution playing field, so price is often perceived as the determinant of value. Therefore, companies are left with only two ways to really add value: through their brand and their relationships with customers and prospects. Switching to a customer-centric system positively influences both.

In reversing the value chain, the customer's needs are your starting point, as it is in the Circle of Traction. By providing superior customer value—delivering a level of quality the customer expects to receive for the price paid for goods and services—companies gain the best opportunity to increase their valuation. Because customer-centric companies are able to achieve a better competitive position, they can realize greater market momentum, market share, return on shareholder equity, and faster growth. Doing things the way you've always done them, living with the status quo—whether this approach is working or not—is always the easy way. We created the Circle of Traction to help you take the actions required to facilitate the transformation to a more customer-centric organization. We hope this book encourages you to use the wheel in your quest to achieve organic growth and long-term success by focusing your efforts on what customers value.

ABOUT THE AUTHOR

LAURA PATTERSON

Laura Patterson is the author of three previous business books: *Gone Fishin': A Guide to Finding, Hooking, Keeping, and Growing Profitable Customers*; *Measure What Matters: Reconnecting Marketing to Business Goals*; and *Marketing Metrics in Action: Creating a Performance-Driven Marketing Organization*. She is known for her practical, no-nonsense approach to proving and improving the value of Marketing.

Laura began her 25+ year career in sales and had the great fortune of working across functions spanning customer relationship management and Marketing with a capital "M." Today she is at the helm of VisionEdge Marketing, founded in 1999, and is recognized as one of the pioneers and authorities in the Marketing Performance Management (MPM) discipline. The company specializes in helping companies apply data, metrics, and proven best-in-class practices to improve Marketing effectiveness, deliver business impact, and enable better business decision-making. Laura and VisionEdge Marketing are all about making Marketing an engine of growth for organizations.

Martechexec selected Laura as one of the top 50 women in marketing technology, and she is honored to be among the Top 20 Women in Business according to the Sales Lead Management Association. Engagio identified her as being among the top Marketing Operations leaders to know. Laura has served on the University of Texas McCombs School of Business Masters of Marketing Science Advisory Board.

Connect with Laura

laurapattersonvem
visionedgemarketing

marketingtransformation

lauravem

laurap@visionedgemarketing.com
fasttrack@visionedgemarketing.com

#FastTrackYourBiz
#CircleofTraction
#FastTrackYourBusiness
#FastTrackYourGrowth

HERE'S HOW WE CAN WORK TOGETHER

From consulting to coaching, work sessions to workbooks, or hands-on collaboration to online DIY tools, VisionEdge Marketing has the services that can help you, no matter your budget.

How you can engage with Laura through VisionEdge Marketing:

- Interactive Marketing Workshops
- Audits, Reviews and Assessments
- Collaborative Consulting
- Keynote Speaking

Discover more, invite Laura to speak at your event, or take your business to the next level by visiting VisionEdgeMarketing.com.

GET YOUR FREE GIFT

EVALUATE YOUR STATE OF READINESS FOR ORGANIC GROWTH

Organic growth is how a company expands through its own business activity. It requires companies to create competitive advantages, differentiate and innovate their product/service offerings, and home in on viable existing and new customer opportunities.

To succeed at organic growth, your company must understand the needs and wants of the market and customers. You must be able to gather and validate the market requirements to create innovation—differentiated solutions, features, and benefits that will resonate with buyers.

Is your company ready to succeed at organic growth? Get Laura's free assessment and find out today. Plus, Laura shares tips for improving your company's readiness.

http://bit.ly/OrganicGrowthAssessment
Password: FastTrack

ACKNOWLEDGMENTS

In every endeavor where I've experienced success, there were always people who provided support, guidance, and inspiration. This book is no exception. My heartfelt gratitude goes out to Kevin Dunworth of Celling Biosciences, Marc Hafner of Revionics, Kevin Jones of Celero Commerce, JT McCormick of Scribe Media, Steve "Ziggy" Shanklin of White Cloud Security, Dave Sikora of ALTR, Greg Stock of Zenoss, Becky Taylor of SensorRX, and other executives who shared their time, insights, and experiences for achieving organic growth and influenced my approach to this book.

This book wouldn't exist without the support my husband, who whether he's serving as teacher, coach, critic, or equipment manager, is always in my court.

Special thanks to Jeniffer Thompson of Monkey C Media and editor Adrienne Moch for being willing to take this book by the hand and make it better.

ABOUT THE REVIEWERS

David A. Altounian, PH. D.

Dr. Altounian is the Associate Dean of Academic Programs and MBA Program Director in the Bill Munday School of Business at St. Edwards University. He is an Associate Professor of Entrepreneurship and teaches in both the undergraduate and graduate programs. He was the founder and former Co-Chairman and CEO of Motion Computing, a leading provider of mobile computing products for vertical markets. Motion was founded in 2001 and acquired by Xplore Technologies in 2015. He also was a founder of iTaggit Inc., an early web 2.0 company focused on item management.

Dr. Altounian has over 30 years of leading marketing and operations organizations in the technology sector with leading companies including Dell, Motorola, Compaq Computer Corporation and Ashton-Tate. He is a partner at the Capital Factory, an entrepreneurial co-working space, incubator, accelerator, and education facility. He is also a board member of the Greater Austin Chamber of Commerce and the Austin Technology Council. Dr. Altounian earned his Ph.D. at Oklahoma State University and his MBA at the Kellogg School of Management at Northwestern University.

Arie Brish

Arie Brish serves his global clients as a ground-breaker in growth strategies, commercialization of new paradigms, change leadership and turn-around. He is also a best seller author of "Lay an Egg and Make Chicken Soup", which is a practical guide for the many moving parts and potential blind spots in commercializing new products and services. It placed #1 New Release, received top-notch five stars reviews, and has ranked among the "Top Ten Best Sellers" in the VC category.

He brings to the table lessons learned and best practices gained from a wide variety of assignments in different industries and across business disciplines. His business acumen includes CEO & GM roles, Board of Directors, M&A, business development, turnarounds and change leadership, working with Fortune 500 corporations, entrepreneurial initiatives, consulting engagements, and non-profits.

Roger Dooley

Roger Dooley is an author, keynote speaker, and podcast host. His books include Friction (McGraw Hill, 2019) and Brainfluence. (Wiley). He writes the popular blog Neuromarketing and a column at Forbes.com. He co-founded College Confidential, the leading college-bound website. Before his entrepreneurial adventures, he held a senior strategy position at a Fortune 1000 company.

Mitch Goozé

A recognized expert in marketing, innovation and leadership, strategic positioning, and customer relationships, Mitch Goozé has addressed groups throughout the world, winning high ratings for his energetic presentation style and results-oriented approach.

Mitch Goozé is an experienced general manager and leader with operating experience in the high technology and consumer products industries. He has experience running divisions of large companies, as well as being CEO of mid-sized companies. Mr. Goozé was president of Teledyne Components, a division of Teledyne, Inc. for five years. He has been a member of Customer Manufacturing Group since 1991.

Matt Heinz

A prolific author and nationally recognized, award-winning blogger, Matt Heinz is President and Founder of Heinz Marketing with 20 years of marketing, business development and sales experience from a variety of organizations and industries. He is a dynamic speaker, memorable not only for his keen insight and humor, but his actionable and motivating takeaways. Matt is a repeat winner of Top 50 Most Influential People in Sales Lead Management and Top 50 Sales & Marketing Influencers.

Theresa Kushner

Theresa Kushner is an accomplished, business-centric data executive, board advisor and published author who leads companies through transformation during rapid technology, regulatory and market disruptions. She brings 25+ of expertise harnessing data and analytics, company and customer information to lower costs and contribute multi-billion dollar growth for technology leaders including Cisco Systems, IBM, VMWare, and Dell/EMC.

Theresa is a member of data.world Advisory Board, where she advises on using data and analytics, using data to measure marketing contributions and on aligning the organization with industry experts. Theresa is a thought leader on data with two co-authored books on the subject. She is a sought-after speaker on data and analytics and a regular contributor to Latin Business Today—also sitting on the Advisory Council to this site. Theresa has been recognized with numerous awards, including the International Institute of Analytics Association Award for VMWare analytics (2016) and Database Marketing Association Award for Excellence from Cisco, among others. Her teams have been awarded seven patents for analytical algorithms developed, IBM, Cisco, and Dell/EMC. She graduated from the Stanford Executive Program in 2016.

Jim Sterne

Jim Sterne sold business computers to first-time owners in the 1980s, consulted and keynoted about online marketing in the 1990s, founded a conference and a professional association around digital analytics in the 2000s and recently published his twelfth book, Artificial Intelligence for Marketing: Practical Applications. Sterne has remained active producing the Marketing Analytics Summit since 2002 and as Director Emeritus of the Digital Analytics Association.

ENDNOTES

1 "Growth Strategy." KPMG. Accessed July 31, 2019. https://home.kpmg/xx/en/home/services/advisory/strategy/our-services/growth-strategy.html.

2 Koetsier, John. "Almost 70% of CEOs Now Expect CMOs to Lead Revenue Growth." VentureBeat. December 16, 2016. Accessed July 31, 2019. https://venturebeat.com/2016/12/16/almost-70-of-ceos-now-expect-cmos-to-lead-revenue-growth/.

3 "Newsroom." Gartner. Accessed July 31, 2019. https://www.gartner.com/en/newsroom.

4 Spangler, Todd, and Todd Spangler. "Hulu Tops 25 Million Subscribers, Claims Nearly $1.5 Billion in 2018 Ad Revenue." Variety. January 08, 2019. Accessed July 31, 2019. https://variety.com/2019/digital/news/hulu-25-million-subscribers-2018-ad-revenue-1203102356/.

5 "Time Warner Growth Comparisons." Time Warner (TWX) Growth Rates Comparisons to Broadcasting Media & Cable TV Industry, Sector, Market. Sales, Income, EPS. Accessed July 31, 2019. https://csimarket.com/stocks/growthrates.php?code=TWX.

6 Wahba, Phil. "Sam's Club CEO: The 63 Stores We Closed Are Fueling E-Commerce Growth." Fortune. September 24, 2018. Accessed July 31, 2019. http://fortune.com/2018/09/24/sams-club-furner-brainstorm-reinvent/.

7 https://www.businesswire.com/news/home/20160309005799/en/Who's-Boss-Workplace-Culture-HR-Managers-Employees.

8 "What We Believe · Forrester." Forrester. Accessed August 08, 2019. https://go.forrester.com/age-of-the-customer/.

9 "Engagement Economy: The Future of Massively Scaled Collaboration and Participation." Institute for the Future. Accessed August 8, 2019. www.iftf.org.

10 "The Business of Data." The Economist Intelligence Unit. Accessed August 8, 2019. https://eiuperspectives.economist.com/sites/default/files/images/Business of Data briefing paper WEB.pdf.

11 "The Definition of Customer Success." Customer Success Association. Accessed August 08, 2019. https://www.customersuccessassociation.com/library/the-definition-of-customer-success/.

12 "Key Findings From the Gartner Customer Experience Survey." Gartner. Accessed August 08, 2019. https://www.gartner.com/en/marketing/insights/articles/key-findings-from-the-gartner-customer-experience-survey.

13 "Digital Trends 2018 Report - In Association with Econsultancy." Adobe. Accessed August 08, 2019. https://www.adobe.com/uk/modal-offers/econsultancy_digital_trends_2018_report.html.

14 "2019 Customer Experience Benchmarking Report." 2019 Customer Experience Benchmarking Report. Accessed August 08, 2019. https://www.dimensiondata.com/en/insights/customer-experience-benchmarking-report-2019.

15 "Customer Experience Defined." Forrester. July 31, 2018. Accessed August 08, 2019. https://go.forrester.com/blogs/definition-of-customer-experience/.

16 "Customer Experience Management: A Revolutionary Approach to Connecting with Your Customers." Amazon. Accessed August 11, 2019. https://www.amazon.com/Customer-Experience-Management-Revolutionary-Connecting/dp/0471237744.

17 Cook, Miles. "How to Choose Tires and Wheels." Edmunds. October 24, 2007. Accessed August 11, 2019. https://www.edmunds.com/how-to/how-to-choose-tires-and-wheels.html.

18 Admin. "The Purpose of Business Is to Make a Difference in the World: 3/4." Virgin. April 27, 2017. Accessed August 10, 2019. https://www.virgin.com/virgin-unite/leadership-and-advocacy/purpose-business-make-difference-world-34.

19 "Why 90% of Enterprise Organizations Say Data and Analytics Are Key to Digital Transformation." Business 2 Community. Accessed August 10, 2019. https://www.business2community.com/big-data/why-90-of-enterprise-organizations-say-data-and-analytics-are-key-to-digital-transformation-02112348.

20 "2018 Global State of Enterprise Analytics Report." MicroStrategy. Accessed August 10, 2019.

21 "Marketing-recordings-videos-webinars." VisionEdge Marketing. June 12, 2019. Accessed August 13, 2019. https://visionedgemarketing.com/marketing-recordings-videos-webinars/.

22 "Deloitte US." Deloitte United States. Accessed August 13, 2019. https://cmo.deloitte.com/xc/en/pages/articles/deloitte-cmo-council-launch-report-on-cmo-revenue-growth.html.

23 Pope, Leah. "Marketers, The Gauntlet Has Been Thrown Down For 2018: Grow Or Go." Forbes. December 27, 2017. Accessed August 13, 2019. https://www.forbes.com/sites/forbescommunicationscouncil/2017/12/27/marketers-the-gauntlet-has-been-thrown-down-for-2018-grow-or-go/#cb4c33f715bb.

24 Ansoff, Igor. "Strategies for Diversification." *Harvard Business Review*, (35) 5, 1957, 113-24.

25 "AT&T Calls New Video Phone Wave of the Future." UPI. January 06, 1992. Accessed August 13, 2019. https://www.upi.com/Archives/1992/01/06/ATT-calls-new-video-phone-wave-of-the-future/8670694674000/.

26 "Living.com Has Died." CNNMoney. Accessed August 13, 2019. https://money.cnn.com/2000/08/15/companies/living_dead/index.htm.

27 Golder, Peter N., and Gerard J. Tellis. "Pioneer Advantage: Marketing Logic or Marketing Legend." American Marketing Association. Accessed August 13, 2019. https://faculty.fuqua.duke.edu/~moorman/Marketing-Strategy-Seminar-2015/Session 5/Golder and Tellis.pdf.

28 "Beating the Odds in Market Entry." McKinsey & Company. Accessed August 13, 2019. https://www.mckinsey.com/business-functions/strategy-and-corporate-finance/our-insights/beating-the-odds-in-market-entry.

29 Moore, James F. "Predators and Prey: A New Ecology of Competition." Harvard Business Review. August 01, 2014. Accessed August 15, 2019. https://hbr.org/1993/05/predators-and-prey-a-new-ecology-of-competition.

30 Worldwide, The Alternative Board. "Why Is Strategic Planning Important?" TAB The Alternative Board Business Coaching Services. Accessed August 14, 2019. https://www.thealternativeboard.com/blog/why-is-strategic-planning-important.

31 Morris, Tricia. "12 Data and Analytics Predictions through 2025." MicroStrategy. June 25, 2018. Accessed August 15, 2019. https://www.microstrategy.com/us/resources/blog/bi-trends/12-data-and-analytics-predictions-through-2025.

32 "Data, Data Everywhere: A Special Report on Managing Information." Accessed August 15, 2019. https://www.emc.com/collateral/analyst-reports/ar-the-economist-data-data-everywhere.pdf.

33 "What We Believe · Forrester." Forrester. Accessed August 15, 2019. https://go.forrester.com/age-of-the-customer/.

34 "Mastering Three Strategies of Organic Growth." McKinsey & Company. Accessed August 15, 2019. https://www.mckinsey.com/business-functions/marketing-and-sales/our-insights/mastering-three-strategies-of-organic-growth.

35 Gambino, Megan. "A Salute to the Wheel." Smithsonian.com. June 17, 2009. Accessed August 15, 2019. https://www.smithsonianmag.com/science-nature/a-salute-to-the-wheel-31805121/.

36 Goss, Jennifer L. "How Henry Ford's Assembly Line Changed Manufacturing." ThoughtCo. July 24, 2019. Accessed August 15, 2019. https://www.thoughtco.com/henry-ford-and-the-assembly-line-1779201.

37 "History of the Automobile." Wikipedia. August 12, 2019. Accessed August 15, 2019. https://en.m.wikipedia.org/wiki/History_of_the_automobile.

38 Papadopoulos, Loukia. "7 Tire Innovations That Will Have Your Mind Reeling." Interesting Engineering. September 24, 2018. Accessed August 15, 2019. https://interestingengineering.com/7-tire-innovations-that-will-have-your-mind-reeling.

39 "Growth & Innovation: Strategy & Corporate Finance." McKinsey & Company. Accessed August 15, 2019. https://www.mckinsey.com/business-functions/strategy-and-corporate-finance/how-we-help-clients/growth-and-innovation.

40 "The Pmarca Guide to Startups." Pmarchive. Accessed August 15, 2019. https://pmarchive.com/guide_to_startups_part4.html.

41 "The Startup Guide to Finding & Measuring Product/Market Fit." Baremetrics. November 01, 2017. Accessed August 15, 2019. https://baremetrics.com/blog/startup-product-market-fit.

42 "Go-to-Market / Product-Market-Fit Checklist." Google Sheets. Accessed August 15, 2019. https://docs.google.com/spreadsheets/d/13tKSM8EdUSFfivEAVcWW3-fJpBGoUmYrWfMJrdSnuqU/edit#gid=0.

43 "Product-market Fit Survey (Sean Ellis)." Always Going North - Notes on Customer Acquisition, Growth, and App Marketing. Accessed August 15, 2019. http://www.alwaysgoingnorth.com/product-market-fit-survey-sean-ellis/.

44 Revolvy, LLC. ""Economic Value to the Customer" on Revolvy.com." Revolvy. Accessed August 17, 2019. https://www.revolvy.com/page/Economic-value-to-the-customer.

45 Michael J. Lanning and Edward G. Michaels, "A Business Is a Value Delivery System," McKinsey Staff Paper no. 41, June 1998, http://www.dpvgroup.com/wp-content/uploads/2009/11/1988-A- Business-is-a-VDS-McK-Staff-Ppr.pdf.

46 "Marketing-recordings-videos-webinars." VisionEdge Marketing. June 12, 2019. Accessed August 16, 2019. https://visionedgemarketing.com/marketing-recordings-videos-webinars/.

47 Trout, Jack. "Differentiate Or Die." Forbes. June 19, 2013. Accessed August 16, 2019. https://www.forbes.com/2005/12/02/ibm-nordstrom-cocacola-cx_jt_1205trout.html#1c6a8e34286e.

48 "New Product Development Process: Stage-Gate International." Stage. July 11, 2019. Accessed August 16, 2019. https://www.stage-gate.com/new-product-development-process/.

49 "Myths About New Product Failure Rates." New Product Success. September 05, 2018. Accessed August 16, 2019. https://newproductsuccess.org/white-papers__trashed/new-product-failure-rates-2013-jpim-30-pp-976-979/.

50 "Up to 95 Percent of New Product Introductions Fail: AcuPOLL." Product Launch. Accessed August 16, 2019. https://productlaunch.typepad.com/product_launch/2007/01/doing_everythin.html.

51 Akrani, Gaurav. "Stages Process Steps of New Product Development." KALYAN CITY LIFE BLOG. Accessed August 17, 2019. https://kalyan-city.blogspot.com/2012/02/stages-process-steps-of-new-product.html.

52 "The Granularity of Growth." McKinsey & Company. Accessed August 17, 2019. https://www.mckinsey.com/featured-insights/employment-and-growth/the-granularity-of-growth.

53 Adams, Rob. "New Book Giveaway!" Inc.com. April 27, 2010. Accessed August 17, 2019. https://www.inc.com/rob-adams/market-validation-new-book.html.

54 Richardson, Adam. "Using Customer Journey Maps to Improve Customer Experience." Harvard Business Review. March 01, 2017. Accessed August 18, 2019. https://hbr.org/2010/11/using-customer-journey-maps-to.

55 "Strategic Initiatives Study: Adapting Corporate Strategy to the Changing Economy." FD|The Strategic Communications Division of FTI Consulting. Accessed August 17, 2019. https://i.forbesimg.com/forbesinsights/StudyPDFs/FD_AdaptingCorporateStrategy.pdf.

56 InsideView Follow. "The State of Sales and Marketing Alignment in 2018." LinkedIn SlideShare. July 28, 2018. Accessed August 19, 2019. https://www.slideshare.net/insideview/the-state-of-sales-and-marketing-alignment-in-2018.

57 "Forrester." B2B Buyers Mandate A New Charter For Marketing And Sales. Accessed August 19, 2019. https://www.forrester.com/report/B2B Buyers Mandate A New Charter For Marketing And Sales/-/E-RES132705#.

58 Aug 10, 2005 Strategic Management Global Focus. "Three Reasons Why Good Strategies Fail: Execution, Execution..." Knowledge@Wharton. Accessed August 17, 2019. https://knowledge.wharton.upenn.edu/article/three-reasons-why-good-strategies-fail-execution-execution/.

59 "Remembering Bill Smith, Father of Six Sigma." ISixSigma. November 27, 2018. Accessed August 18, 2019. https://www.isixsigma.com/new-to-six-sigma/history/remembering-bill-smith-father-six-sigma/.

60 "The High Performance Organization (HPO) Framework." HPO Center. Accessed August 18, 2019. https://www.hpocenter.com/hpo-framework/.

61 "Bureaucratic Theory Definition by Max Weber." ToolsHero. November 05, 2018. Accessed August 19, 2019. https://www.toolshero.com/management/bureaucratic-theory-weber/.

62 Taylor, Frederick Winslow. "The Principles of Scientific Management." Amazon. July 08, 1997. Accessed August 19, 2019. https://www.amazon.com/Principles-Scientific-Management-Frederick-Winslow/dp/0486299880.

63 "Concept of the Corporation › Customer Reviews." Amazon. Accessed August 19, 2019. https://www.amazon.com/Concept-Corporation-Peter-F-Drucker/product-reviews/1560006250.

64 Senge, Peter M. "The Fifth Discipline: The Art & Practice of The Learning Organization." Amazon. Accessed August 19, 2019. https://www.amazon.com/Fifth-Discipline-Practice-Learning-Organization/dp/0385517254.

65 "Marketing-recordings-videos-webinars." VisionEdge Marketing. June 12, 2019. Accessed August 18, 2019. https://visionedgemarketing.com/marketing-recordings-videos-webinars-2/.

66 "Managing Performance." Amazon. September 30, 2004. Accessed August 19, 2019. https://www.amazon.com/Managing-Performance-Angela-Baron/dp/1843981017.

67 "What Is Customer Retention? Definition and Metrics." NGDATA. July 03, 2018. Accessed August 18, 2019. https://www.ngdata.com/what-is-customer-retention/.

68 "Marketing-recordings-videos-webinars." VisionEdge Marketing. June 12, 2019. Accessed August 18, 2019. https://visionedgemarketing.com/marketing-recordings-videos-webinars-2/.

69 Franco-Santos, Monica. "The Performance Impact of Using Measurement Diversity in Executives' Annual Incentive Systems." Semantic Scholar. 2007. Accessed August 19, 2019. https://pdfs.semanticscholar.org/ad83/b8d600e50b1ba9b5b168e04db3036d12795e.pdf.

70 Kaplan, Robert S., and David P. Norton. "The Balanced Scorecard: Translating Strategy into Action." Amazon. September 01, 1996. Accessed August 19, 2019. https://www.amazon.com/Balanced-Scorecard-Translating-Strategy-Action/dp/0875846513.

71 Lee, Ju-Yeon, Conor M. Henderson, Shrihari Sridhar, and Robert Palmatier. "Effect of Customer-Centric Structure on Long-Term Financial Performance." ResearchGate. March 2015. Accessed August 21, 2019. https://www.researchgate.net/publication/265306624_Effect_of_Customer-Centric_Structure_on_Long-Term_Financial_Performance.

72 "Explaining Customer Centricity With a Diagram." LinkedIn. Accessed August 21, 2019. https://www.linkedin.com/pulse/20130123164215-17102372-explaining-customer-centricity-with-a-diagram/.

73 Bhalla, Roland T. RustChristine MoormanGaurav. "Rethinking Marketing." Harvard Business Review. July 16, 2015. Accessed August 21, 2019. https://hbr.org/2010/01/rethinking-marketing.

74 "Customer-centricity: Embedding It into Your Organisation's DNA." Deloitte. 2014. Accessed August 21, 2019. https://www2.deloitte.com/content/dam/Deloitte/ie/Documents/Strategy/2014_customer_centricity_deloitte_ireland.pdf.

75 Egol, Matthew, Paul Hyde, Frank Ribeiro, and Andrew Tipping. "The Customer-Centric Organization: From Pushing Products to Winning Customers." Strategy&. 2004. Accessed August 21, 2019. https://www.strategyand.pwc.com/media/file/The_Customer_Centric_Organization.pdf.

INDEX

NOTE: Page references in *italics* refer to figures.

CPSIA information can be obtained
at www.ICGtesting.com
Printed in the USA
BVHW060733210120
569692BV00005B/20

9 780971 008625